THE BIOLOGICAL ROLE OF RIBONUCLEIC ACIDS

WEIZMANN MEMORIAL LECTURES
Yad Chaim Weizmann, Rehovoth

December 1953
ROBERT ROBINSON
The Structural Relations of Natural Products
Oxford University Press, 1955

December 1954
P. M. S. BLACKETT
Lectures on Rock Magnetism
Weizmann Science Press, 1956

November 1955
E. B. CHAIN
Recent Advances in the Field of Antibiotics
Weizmann Science Press, in preparation

December 1955
C. K. WEBSTER
The Founder of the National Home
Weizmann Science Press, 1956

May 1958
C. K. INGOLD
Substitution at Elements other than Carbon
Weizmann Science Press, 1959

April 1959
J. BRACHET
The Biological Role of Ribonucleic Acids
Elsevier Publishing Company, 1960

THE BIOLOGICAL ROLE

OF

RIBONUCLEIC ACIDS

Sixth Weizmann Memorial Lecture Series

April 1959

by

JEAN BRACHET

Faculty of Sciences, University of Brussels, Belgium

ELSEVIER PUBLISHING COMPANY

AMSTERDAM   LONDON   NEW YORK   PRINCETON

1960

SOLE DISTRIBUTORS FOR THE UNITED STATES OF NORTH AMERICA:
D. VAN NOSTRAND COMPANY, INC.
120 Alexander Street, Princeton, N.J. (Principal office)
24 West 40th Street, New York 18, N.Y.

SOLE DISTRIBUTORS FOR CANADA:
D. VAN NOSTRAND COMPANY (CANADA), LTD.
25 Hollinger Road, Toronto 16

SOLE DISTRIBUTORS FOR THE BRITISH COMMONWEALTH EXCLUDING CANADA:
D. VAN NOSTRAND COMPANY, LTD.
358 Kensington High Street, London, W. 14

Library of Congress Catalog Card Number: 60-15524

With 41 figures

PRINTED IN THE NETHERLANDS BY
N.V. DRUKKERIJ G. J. THIEME, NIJMEGEN

Preface

It was both a considerable honour and a great pleasure for the author to be invited to deliver one of the famous Chaïm Weizmann Memorial Lectures at the Weizmann Institute in Rehovoth in April 1959. The high achievements of Chaïm Weizmann, both as a statesman and a scientist, make it difficult for any lecturer to give Memorial lectures which are really worthy of his memory. Furthermore, the extremely high quality, as scientists and as men, of the former Chaïm Weizmann Memorial Lecturers has made the task still more difficult for the present lecturer. In fact, the greatest tribute which a scientist can pay to Weizmann's memory is to visit, to admire and to love his country and the Institute which bears his name in Rehovoth: he will find in the Institute the great qualities of intellect, good organization and humanity which make the charm and the greatness of Israël. For allowing him to make such a visit to Israël, the author will always remain thankful to his colleagues and friends of the Weizmann Institute.

The present book is the presentation in written form of the last Chaïm Weizmann Lectures; there were three lectures which dealt respectively with: *(1)* Ribonucleic acids and protein synthesis; *(2)* The role of ribonucleic acids in growth and morphogenesis; *(3)* The role of the cell nucleus in ribonucleic acid and protein synthesis. Each of these lectures is presented here as a separate chapter, the title of the whole book being: The Biological Role of Ribonucleic Acids. The author wishes to acknowledge the fact that part of the material presented here has already been published in his two previous books: *Biochemical Cytology* (Academic Press, New York, 1957) and *The Biochemistry of Development* (Pergamon Press, London, 1960). He also wishes to express his sincere thanks to his secretaries, Mrs. E. De Saedeleer and Mrs. Y. Thomas, for their efficient help in the publication of the manuscript and the preparation of the index.

Brussels   J. BRACHET
September 1960

Contents

Chapter 1

Ribonucleic Acids and Protein Synthesis

1. BRIEF HISTORICAL SURVEY

Next to nothing was known a quarter of a century ago about the biological role and the intracellular localization of the nucleic acids. All that was well established was the existence of two different types of nucleic acids, which correspond to the deoxyribonucleic (DNA) and ribonucleic (RNA) acids of the present day. They were called, respectively, thymonucleic and zymonucleic acids, because purified preparations had only been obtained from thymus and yeast. It was erroneously believed that thymonucleic acid (DNA) is specific to animal cells and that yeast nucleic acid (RNA) is present only in plant cells. However RNA had been isolated from pancreas. A popular hypothesis was that DNA, which was known to contain both ortho-phosphoric acid and nitrogenous bases, might play the role of an intra-nuclear buffer. Such a role is certainly a minor one for the bearer of "genetic information"!

One of the first important advances made in the field came from cytochemistry, when in 1924 Feulgen and Rossenbeck designed and utilized their well-known reaction for the detection of DNA. They were immediately able to demonstrate that thymonucleic acid (DNA) is specifically located in the cell nucleus, in plants as well as in animals.

Progress on the role and localization of RNA was slower to come, because of the lack of specific cytochemical reactions comparable to the Feulgen tests. Indirect observations by Brachet (1933) strongly suggested, however, that animal cells may contain such

References p. 50/54

large amounts of RNA as to exclude the possibility that *all* of this RNA is localized in the cell nucleus. These observations were made on sea urchin eggs, which had been studied by Needham and Needham a little earlier (1930). They found that there is no increase of "nucleic acid phosphorus" during development, although the number of nuclei increases tremendously. They concluded that DNA must be present in large amounts in the cytoplasm of the unfertilized eggs and that it migrates from the cytoplasm to the nucleus when the latter multiplies. But the combined use of the Feulgen reaction and the specific method of Dische for DNA estimation clearly showed that DNA is not present in large amounts in the cytoplasm of unfertilized sea urchin eggs and that there is considerable synthesis of this nucleic acid during development. It was therefore postulated that, during cleavage, DNA is synthesized at the expense of a reserve of cytoplasmic RNA ("conversion" hypothesis) and it could, in fact, be demonstrated that unfertilized sea urchin eggs contain large amounts of RNA (Brachet, 1933). More than 25 years have elapsed since these experiments were made and one may wonder how much truth there was in the ideas presented at that time by the Needhams and Brachet. It is beyond the scope of the present lectures, which deal with the biological role of RNA, to go into the still obscure question of DNA synthesis in developing eggs. The interested reader will find a full account of the problem in the author's two recent books (Brachet 1957, 1960). It can be said, however, that there is no doubt that DNA is synthesized during development and that unfertilized eggs contain a RNA store; but it is now unlikely that RNA is *directly* converted into DNA and the nature of the precursors used for DNA synthesis in developing eggs remains controversial. Part of the DNA present in the nuclei might come from a small reserve of DNA already present in the unfertilized egg; but it is likely that the main part of the DNA is synthesized at the expense of soluble deoxyribo- and ribonucleosides or nucleotides present in the acid soluble fraction.

Many unsuccessful attempts were made by the author, around 1935, to detect the localization of RNA in unfertilized eggs with the basic dye methyl green. This dye was said to stain nucleic acids in

CYTOCHEMICAL OBSERVATIONS

a specific manner; but even in sea urchin eggs or pancreas, only the nuclei—because of their high DNA content—took the stain. When, as recommended long ago by Unna, a second basic dye (pyronine) is added to methyl green, bright red staining of the cytoplasm and nucleoli occurs. However, it took several years before the real meaning of this staining with pyronine became clear. Purified ribonuclease, *i.e.* the enzyme which breaks down RNA, became available around 1938 and it thus became possible to treat sections with solutions of the crystalline enzyme. As can be seen from a comparison between Figs. 1, 2 (pp. 9, 10), digestion of RNA with ribonuclease leads to the complete disappearance of cytoplasmic and nucleolar basophilia, without at all affecting the staining of chromatin with methyl green. Development of a refined method of UV microspectrophotometry by Caspersson (1936, 1940) led, at the same time, to similar developments. Nucleic acids, because of the presence in their molecule of purine and pyrimidine bases, have a strong absorption in the UV. It was soon found by Caspersson that the cytoplasm and the nucleoli of the cells which have a high RNA content display strong UV absorption, despite the fact that they are Feulgen-negative: RNA must thus be localized primarily in the cytoplasm and the nucleolus.

These early cytochemical studies have led, as we shall see, to the unexpected conclusion that RNA must play a role in protein synthesis. After a brief survey of the results obtained by cytochemical and biochemical methods, more direct evidence, derived from studies on plant viruses, on the action of ribonuclease on living cells and on purified enzyme systems will be presented. These studies lead to the same conclusion, *i.e.* that RNA plays a major and direct role in the synthesis of specific proteins.

2. CYTOCHEMICAL OBSERVATIONS

As we have just pointed out, the conclusion that RNA is somehow concerned with protein synthesis comes from the cytochemical observations of Caspersson (1941) and Brachet (1942). Using entirely different methods for RNA detection, they reached the same conclusion independently and simultaneously.

References p. 50/54

As was shown first by Caspersson and Schultz (1938), RNA is abundant in rapidly growing cells (onion root-tips, imaginal discs of *Drosophila* larvae). Proliferating tissues, however, are by no means the only ones to contain large amounts of RNA in their cytoplasm and nucleoli. The same holds true for the exocrine parts of the pancreas (Fig. 3, p. 11), the cells producing pepsin in the gastric mucosa (Fig. 4, p. 12), liver cells, nerve cells, young oöcytes and embryos undergoing differentiation, all of which are sites of marked protein synthesis. On the other hand, many tissues which have a very high physiological activity, but which do not synthesize large amounts of proteins, contain only small amounts of RNA: such is the case for heart, muscle, or kidney (Caspersson, 1941). Microorganisms, which multiply very rapidly, and thus very quickly synthesize their own proteins (*e.g.*, yeasts or bacteria) are very rich in RNA (Caspersson and Brandt, 1941). In conclusion, all the organs which synthesize large amounts of proteins, whether for growth or multiplication, are always rich in RNA, which is localized in the nucleolus and the cytoplasm. All other cells and tissues have a much lower content in RNA and much less conspicuous nucleoli.

Further confirmatory evidence may be cited. One of the organs which has the largest RNA content is the silk gland in silk worms (Brachet, 1941; Denucé, 1952), the only known function of which is the production of the protein silk. While endocrine glands are relatively poor in RNA, it is a striking fact that stimulation of hormonal secretion in the pituitary is linked with a marked increase in the RNA content (Desclin, 1940; Herlant, 1943; Abolins, 1952).

There is thus no doubt that the RNA content of various cells can be made to vary under different physiological conditions, but always in relation to protein synthesis.

There is, further, more recent evidence for this conclusion. The effect of hypophysectomy and growth hormone on liver cells (Di Stefano *et al.*, 1952, 1955; Fiala *et al.*, 1956), the normal growth and compensatory hypertrophy of the kidney (Kurnick, 1955), the action of cold on neurons (Gordon and Nurnberger, 1955), the growth of feathers (Koning and Hamilton, 1954), and the secretory cycle in pancreas (Oram, 1955), etc., have been studied and a close correlation between RNA content and protein synthesis has been found. The same is also true for plant cells. For instance, in roots of *Vicia faba* (Jensen, 1955) and in the alga *Acetabularia*, the RNA content of the nucleolus decreases when the organism stops growing after it has been left in the dark for some weeks (Stich, 1951). Of interest, in the same respect, is a report of Turian (1956), who concludes that heteroauxin awakens the activity of the RNA system for protein synthesis.

This series of examples clearly shows that we are dealing with a very general phenomenon, which occurs in all living organisms, even when they are submitted to abnormal experimental conditions. One objection could, however, be made. Although cytochemical methods can give an idea of the RNA content of the cell, they yield no information about the rate of protein synthesis. It was logical for Caspersson (1941) and Brachet (1942) to think that gland cells or rapidly dividing cells are the site of extensive protein synthesis, but it must be admitted that no proof of that contention was given at that time.

It is for this reason that, in collaboration with Dr. Ficq, we tried to establish a correlation between basophilia and incorporation of labeled phenylalanine in the various organs of the mouse (Ficq and Brachet, 1956). By combining Unna staining with a track autoradiography method, it was possible to show that, in short-time experiments, there is an excellent correlation between the intensity of pyronine staining and the incorporation of the labeled amino acid into the proteins. As shown in Fig. 5 (p. 13), the strongly basophilic exocrine pancreas shows much greater incorporation of the labeled phenylalanine into its proteins than the islets of Langerhans which are poorer in RNA. Heart muscle, as one might expect from its low basophilia, shows very little radioactivity (Fig. 6, p. 14). Similar observations with the same method were made on reticulocytes by Gavosto and Rechenmann (1954). They found that RNA content and incorporation of glycine into proteins decrease simultaneously during red blood cell formation.

Results almost identical to those of Ficq and Brachet (1956) have been independently reported by Niklas and Oehlert (1956), who used different methods and precursors. For their extensive investigations on mouse, rat, and rabbit, they used ³⁵S-labeled amino acids (instead of phenylalanine) and a stripping film autoradiography method (instead of the track autoradiography method). Nevertheless, they also found that incorporation is highest in protein-producing glands (pancreas, gastric mucosa, reticuloendothelial cells, neurons). Next come tissues where mitotic activity is important (Lieberkühn's glands, *stratum germinativum* of the skin, spermatogonia, follicle cells of the ovary). In the least active tissues (muscle, connective tissue), incorporation is only one-fifthieth of that in the protein-secreting glands. Niklas and Oehlert (1956) conclude that, without any exception, RNA content and incorporation of amino acids into proteins show excellent parallelism. It is also worth mentioning that mature spermatozoa, which contain no RNA, are unable to incorporate amino acids into their proteins (Martin and Brachet, 1959).

However, it would not be correct to believe that all RNA is always metabolically active. For instance, in amphibian ovaries, strongly basophilic degenerating oöcytes are occasionally found. They are almost inert as regards incorporation of amino acids into proteins (Ficq, 1955). Similarly, the testes of mammals often contain a large number of extracellular basophilic bodies. These probably correspond to the extrusion of cytoplasmic RNA during spermiogenesis. These "residual bodies" show very little, if any, activity for amino acid incorporation. Thus the mere presence of RNA is not enough to stimulate protein anabolism. The RNA itself must be in a metabolically active form, probably related to its architecture at the molecular level.

The evidence arising from cytochemistry is thus very striking. However, cytochemical methods do not have the same high degree of accuracy and specificity as straight biochemical techniques and it thus becomes important to find out whether the cytochemical evidence is confirmed by quantitative chemical analyses of the RNA content.

3. QUANTITATIVE CONFIRMATIONS

A large number of independent investigations show clearly that there is a good correlation between the basophilia or ultraviolet absorption of different tissues and their RNA content. This parallelism has already been pointed out by Brachet, who, in 1941, estimated the RNA content of various tissues. Later, better methods were devised for the determination of RNA, but the initial conclusions were not altered. Extensive reviews of the whole question have been given by Davidson (1947, 1953), who made important personal contributions to the subject and who came to the conclusion that the nucleic acid content of different tissues, as determined by chemical methods, is generally in accordance with the values which might be expected on histological grounds.

It was thus found, as expected, that glandular organs, which synthesize large amounts of proteins (pancreas, salivary glands, gastric and intestinal mucosae) are rich in RNA. The same is true to a somewhat smaller degree of organs where mitoses are frequent (spleen, thymus, lymph nodes, testis, various tumors); kidney, brain, heart and lung have a much lower RNA content (see the review of Leslie, 1955, for further information).

We have seen that there is strong cytochemical evidence for the view that the RNA content of cells may vary with changes in physiological conditions, and that these variations are apparently linked to modifications in the rate of protein synthesis. Many quantitative measurements support this view. In liver, for instance, fasting or administration of a protein-poor diet is followed by a decrease in basophilia and a parallel drop in the RNA content (Brachet *et al.*, 1946, Davidson, 1947; Mandel *et al.*, 1950; Campbell and Kosterlitz, 1952; Mirsky *et al.*, 1954; Laird *et al.*, 1955; Stenram, 1954; and others).

The existence of a close quantitative relationship between RNA content and protein synthesis is particularly impressive in growing cultures of micro-organisms. Bacteria, which undergo a very rapid synthesis of their own proteins during growth, are extremely rich in RNA. Values up to 11.5% dry weight have been reported by Vendrely (1946).

Work carried out in several different laboratories shows the existence of an excellent correlation between the synthesis of RNA and the synthesis of proteins, provided that the bacterial growth is studied during the logarithmic phase. For instance, Caldwell *et al.* (1950) found the RNA content of bacteria to be proportional to the growth rate, whatever the experimental conditions (changes in the nitrogen source of the culture medium, presence or absence of inhibitors, normal organisms or slow-growing mutants). Similar findings have been reported by Northrop (1953), Wade (1952) and Price (1952).

An important study of Gale and Folkes (1953) shows that staphylococci synthesize proteins in the presence of glucose and amino acids. If purines and pyrimidines are added to this medium, nucleic acids are also synthesized. But the interesting fact is that if the medium contains no amino acids there is no nucleic acid synthesis, whereas the presence of purines and pyrimidines in the medium enhances protein synthesis. There thus exists a strong positive correlation between the nucleic acid content of the cells and the rate of protein synthesis.

Gale and Folkes (1953) have also found that protein synthesis and RNA synthesis can be dissociated by the use of antibiotics. For instance, chloromycetin, aureomycin, and terramycin all inhibit protein synthesis but increase nucleic acid synthesis. However, there is very good evidence (Neidhardt and Gros, 1957) for the view that the RNA formed in the presence of the antibiotics is abnormal in many respects; it is therefore not surprising that it cannot support protein synthesis. We have already seen that the same situation can be found in the ovary and testis by autoradiography.

The very great importance of the culture conditions in experiments on microorganisms cannot be overemphasized. As was shown very clearly by Jeener (1952, 1953), the relationship between RNA content and protein synthesis is very different in the case of the flagellate *Polytomella coeca*, whether one is dealing with a continuous culture (in exponential phase of growth) or not. If cells are compared during the various stages of growth of a culture, there

Text continued on p. 17

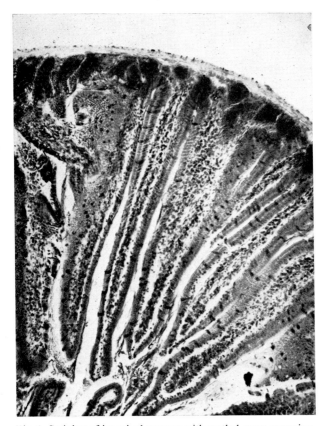

Fig. 1. Staining of intestinal mucosa with methyl green-pyronine.

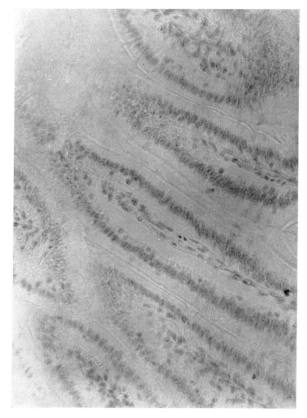

Fig. 2. Staining of intestinal mucosa with methyl green-pyronine after ribonuclease digestion. Only the nuclei are stained.

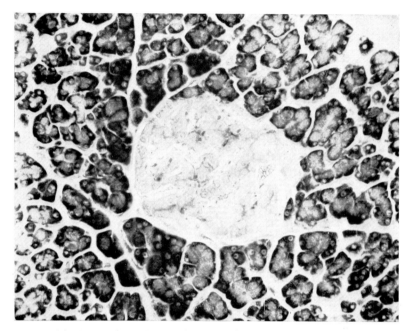

Fig. 3. Exocrine and endocrine parts of pancreas. Unna staining.

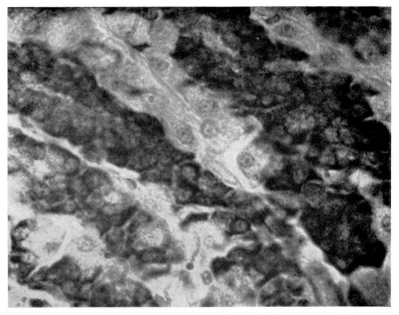

Fig. 4. Gastric mucosa: the pepsin-producing cells show strong staining.
Unna staining.

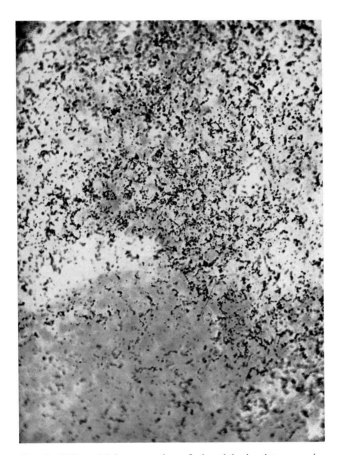

Fig. 5. Differential incorporation of phenylalanine into exocrine (above) and endocrine (below) parts of pancreas (Ficq and Brachet, 1956).

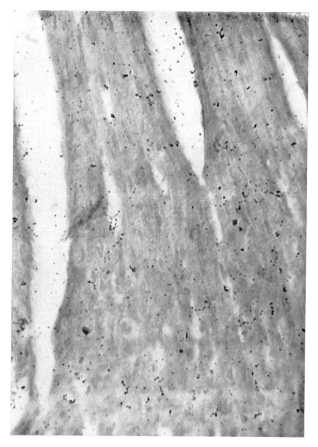

Fig. 6. Very small incorporation of phenylalanine into the
RNA-poor heart muscle (Ficq and Brachet, 1956).

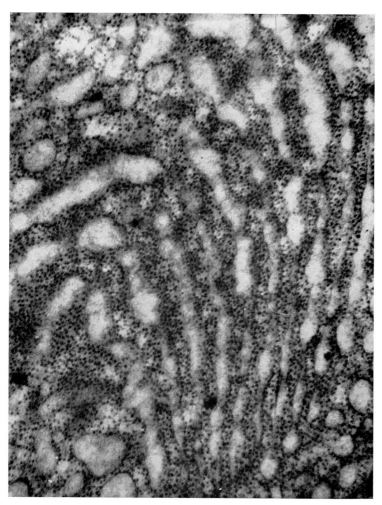

Fig. 7. Electron micrograph of Porter's endoplasmic reticulum at high magnification, showing Palade's small granules (courtesy of Dr. F. Haguenau).

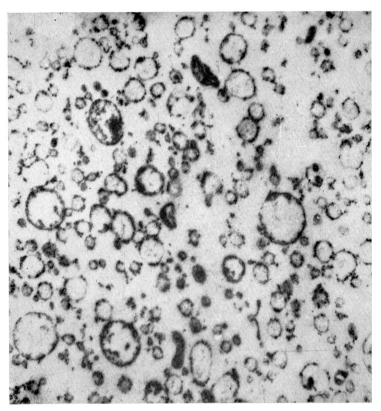

Fig. 8. Electron micrograph of a section through a pellet of microsomes
(courtesy of Dr. Y. Moulé).

is no linear relationship between the quantity of RNA per milligram of protein nitrogen and the rate of protein synthesis (Jeener, 1952). If, on the other hand, continuous cultures are used under conditions where growth maintains itself during long periods at a constant rate which can be varied at will between wide limits, a strict relationship is found between the rate of protein synthesis and the quantity of RNA in excess of a constant basal figure always present in the cells. Thus the close relationship between the quantity of RNA present and protein synthesis exists only for systems in the steady state. When the physiological conditions of the cells are changing rapidly, for instance at the end of the lag and logarithmic phases of growth, no such simple correlation can be found (Jeener, 1953).

There is further work on microorganisms which strongly suggests that protein synthesis and RNA synthesis are closely linked. DNA synthesis, on the other hand, can be dissociated by various means from RNA and protein synthesis.

For instance, Jeener and Jeener (1952) have been able, in the case of Thermobacterium acidophilus, to interfere selectively with either RNA or DNA synthesis by removal from the culture medium of uracil and DNA respectively. In the absence of DNA, the cells still grow as elongated filamentous forms, but the number of bacterial nuclei remains small. In cultures deprived of uracil, growth is inhibited and both nuclei and cytoplasm are affected. These findings indicate that while protein synthesis is dependent on RNA synthesis it is much less directly related to DNA synthesis.

This analysis has been carried one step further by Cohen and Barner (1954, 1955), who worked with quantitative methods on a thymine-requiring mutant of Escherichia coli. They found that in the absence of thymine this organism becomes incapable of forming colonies. This sort of sterilization is accompanied by a marked increase in bacterial length and girth; the RNA content doubles, while there is almost no DNA synthesis. Nevertheless, the organism is still capable of induced enzyme synthesis (synthesis of xylose isomerase, when xylose is added to the medium as an inducer). Synthesis of RNA, protein, and induced enzyme all run parallel in this system in which DNA synthesis has been suppressed. Cohen

References p. 50/54

and Barner's (1954, 1955) conclusions have been confirmed by Ben-Ishai and Volcani (1956), who found that in thymine-less *E. coli* there is a constant ratio between protein synthesis and RNA synthesis. Inhibition of RNA synthesis leads to an inhibition of protein synthesis, but the reverse is not true. It is thus to be concluded that protein synthesis is dependent on RNA synthesis.

Interesting results which lead to similar conclusions have also been obtained with UV-irradiated bacteria. Experiments of Kelner (1953) and of Kanazir and Errera (1954) show that low doses of UV radiation have little effect on RNA and protein synthesis; while they completely stop DNA synthesis, the result again being the production of filamentous bacteria. Ultraviolet irradiation also inhibits the induced synthesis of galactozymase in yeasts (Swenson, 1950; Halvorson and Jackson, 1956). The latter conclude that DNA synthesis in yeasts can be inhibited by UV doses which do not stop RNA and protein synthesis. The UV doses which inhibit the induced synthesis of glucosidase also inhibit the incorporation of glycine into RNA and protein. Ultraviolet light, as well as amino acid analogues, are especially effective in preventing the synthesis of glucosidase, when applied during the latent period which precedes the actual synthesis. Both apparently act on some precursor system, in which RNA seems to be involved.

Still more relevant is Price's (1952) finding that, while staphylococci adapt to lactose, protein synthesis never occurs without a simultaneous increase in RNA. His observations strongly suggest that the synthesis of a new enzyme is linked to the synthesis of new RNA molecules.

This last suggestion has recently received a good deal of attention, especially in Pardee's (1954, 1955) and Spiegelman's (1955) laboratories. Pyrimidine-requiring mutants of *E. coli* can synthesize induced enzymes only when the medium is supplemented with the required bases. Pardee's experiments (1954, 1955) lead him to the conclusion that continuous production of new RNA molecules is necessary for induced enzyme synthesis, and that the bulk of bacterial RNA is inert in this process. Furthermore, Pardee and Prestidge (1955) found experimental conditions in which both RNA and protein synthesis were inhibited while DNA synthesis remained unimpaired.

Similar conclusions have been drawn by Spiegelman and his co-workers (1955) from a series of extensive experiments on induced enzyme synthesis. They found that strong interference with DNA synthesis has no striking effect on enzyme formation, whereas a 50% inhibition of RNA synthesis completely suppresses induced enzyme synthesis.

Recent experiments of Chantrenne (1956a, b) confirm in a very convincing way that the synthesis of a specific enzyme protein is associated with the synthesis of a new, possibly specific RNA. He found that, when non-respiring yeast cells synthesize catalase under the inducing action of oxygen, new RNA molecules are built up. Under Chantrenne's (1956a, b) experimental conditions, adenine is incorporated into RNA of adapting cells at a faster rate than in non-adapted cells; furthermore, this incorporation occurs preferentially in one particular cell fraction.

The evidence, as it now stands, is thus strongly in favor of the idea that, in microorganisms, fresh RNA synthesis occurs whenever new protein synthesis has been induced.

4. THE ROLE OF THE MICROSOMES AND
RIBONUCLEOPROTEIN PARTICLES IN PROTEIN SYNTHESIS

We have already seen that RNA is mainly localized in the nucleolus and in the cytoplasm. A little more will be said now about cytoplasmic RNA, while the subject of nuclear RNA will be left for Chapter 3.

Thanks to the pioneer work of Claude (1943), it is known that the bulk of cytoplasmic RNA, in a homogenate, is associated with small particles, *the microsomes*. Electron microscopy has helped considerably in our understanding of the real nature of these microsomes (see Brachet, 1957, and Haguenau, 1958, for detailed reviews of the question). In short, the microsomes present in a homogenate are breakdown products of elaborate cytoplasmic structures, known to electron microscopists as the *endoplasmic reticulum* or *ergastoplasm.* As can be seen in Fig. 7 (p. 15), these structures —which are particularly well developed in gland cells—are essentially a system of double membranes, in which small granules (often called Palade's granules) are embedded. There is good evidence for the view that the membranes are made of proteins associated with lipids, while the small granules contain RNA. When the cell is homogenized, the ergastoplasm breaks down into small fragments, which are the microsomes (Fig. 8, p. 16). Palade's granules are still attached to remnants of the double membranes, which now form vesicles of various sizes. It has been found recently that it is possible, by treatment of a homogenate with bile salts, to separate the granules from the rest of the microsomes. Deoxycholate, for instance, dissolves the membranes and, on prolonged ultracentrifugation, the granules can be collected. Since they are very rich in RNA, they are usually called "small ribonucleoprotein particles".

If RNA really plays an essential part in protein synthesis, one would of course expect the microsomes and ribonucleoprotein particles to be very active sites of protein synthesis. We shall now see that this expectation has been fulfilled.

Already, in their first papers on the chemical composition of cytoplasmic particles, Brachet and Jeener (1944) pointed out that there is no reason to believe that RNA alone plays a part in protein synthesis: it is quite possible that the whole granule, the microsome, is the active agent.

They found some support for this hypothesis in the fact that particles obtained in the ultracentrifuge (which were in fact mixtures of mitochondria and microsomes) always contained an appreciable amount of the specific protein synthesized by each organ. This was found to be the case for trypsin and insulin in the pancreas, amylase in salivary glands, hemoglobin in red blood cells, and the melanophore-expanding hormone in the pituitary. More recently, Daly *et al.* (1955) confirmed that an appreciable proportion of protease and amylase is bound to the microsomes in pancreas.

Much more direct evidence has come from work done in other laboratories with labeled amino acids. Borsook *et al.* (1950) were the first to report that incorporation in liver tissue is highest in the microsomes after intravenous injection of labeled amino acids (glycine, lysine and leucine). The same result was also obtained by Hultin (1950), who used glycine-^{15}N and worked with the chick. The uptake *in vivo* of the amino acid by the microsomal protein took place more rapidly than in any other fraction, including mitochondria and nuclei. He concluded that a high RNA concentration, which is characteristic of the microsomes, is more important for protein synthesis than the energy-producing systems present in the mitochondria.

Later work by Tyner *et al.* (1952) with glycine-^{14}C, by Keller (1951) with labeled leucine, and by Lee *et al.* (1951) with cystine-^{35}S, all in the rat, quickly confirmed these early results. The same conclusion, *i.e.* that incorporation is greater in microsomal protein than in all other cellular fractions, has also been reached by Smellie *et al.* (1953), who worked with formate-^{14}C, glycine-^{15}N and methionine-^{35}S, by Hendler (1959), who studied the oviduct of the hen, and by Rabinovitz and Olson (1956) for reticulocytes.

Work on the homogenates *in vitro* also confirms the exceptional activity of the microsomal fraction in the incorporation of amino acids. Such work has been done by Borsook *et al.* (1950) and by Siekevitz (1952), who both emphasized, however, the importance of energy-yielding reactions for successful incorporation *in vitro*. For instance, Siekevitz (1952) found that incorporation of labeled alanine by liver homogenates requires the presence of both mitochondria and microsomes, the activity being greatest in the latter. The uptake is greatly increased by the addition of α-ketoglutarate to the system, while dinitrophenol is greatly inhibitory. The incorporation is thus linked to energy production through oxidative phosphorylation.

In a return to the *in vivo* experiments, Allfrey *et al.* (1953, 1955a, b) found that there is a close correlation between the RNA content of the microsome fraction pellet and the rate of protein synthesis in a tissue, and that in pancreas the protein pellet serves as a precursor material in the synthesis of the secretory proteins. Similar conclusions have been reached by Siekevitz and Palade (1958) who also worked on pancreas, and by Oota and Osawa (1954) and Martin and Morton (1956), who worked on plant material. It thus seems to be a general property of all living organisms that microsomes, probably because of their high RNA content, play an exceedingly important role in protein synthesis. Experiments by Allfrey *et al.* (1953) and by Zamecnik and Keller (1954) have given proof that RNA is directly involved in the incorporation of amino acids into the proteins of the microsomes: adding ribonuclease strongly inhibits the *in vitro* incorporation process. According to Zamecnik and Keller (1954), all that is required for the incorporation are microsomes with intact RNA, a non-dialyzable soluble fraction, and an ATP-generating system. We shall return to this point later in this chapter. We have seen that the microsomes can be disintegrated by deoxycholate, with the

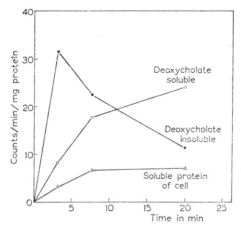

Fig. 9. Incorporation *in vivo* of leucine into the two components of the microsomes and into the soluble protein of the cell (Littlefield *et al.*, 1955).

liberation of small ribonucleoprotein particles (about 240 Å diameter) as a result. According to Littlefield *et al.* (1955) and Zamecnik *et al.* (1956), these small granules, which contain as much as 44% RNA and can be considered as simple nucleoproteins, are seven to eight times more active as regards amino acid incorporation than the deoxycholate-soluble material from the microsomes (Fig. 9).

A similar fraction has also been obtained from ascites tumor cells by Littlefield and Keller (1957). Here again, the small granules are several times more active than the microsomes, and the incorporation process is inhibited by ribonuclease. Full activity requires the presence of ATP, guanosine triphosphate and a soluble enzyme fraction (which will be discussed later). The facts that the small RNA-rich granules are more active than the whole microsomes and that ribonuclease has inhibitory effects leave little doubt that RNA is *directly* concerned in the incorporation mechanism; the latter is considered by Littlefield *et al.* (1955) as an irreversible step in protein synthesis.

The question of the role of the microsomes in protein synthesis of plant cells has been the object of several interesting studies. According to Stephenson and Zamecnik (1956), the microsomes of leaves are no more active than other cell fractions. Only the chloroplasts can incorporate amino acids into their proteins *in vitro*, provided that oxygen and light are supplied. But, in more recent experiments, Stephenson *et al.* (1956) come to the conclusion that in tobacco leaves microsomes are, as in animal cells, initial sites of incorporation of amino acids into proteins.

While the respective roles of the chloroplasts and the microsomes in protein synthesis remain obscure, there is no doubt that in plant cells which are free of chloroplasts the microsomes play the same role as in animal cells. The experiments of Webster and Johnson (1955) are very impressive in proving this point. Studying incorporation of amino acids in a particulate portion of pea roots, which is homologous to the microsome fraction, Webster (1955) and Webster and Johnson (1955) found the process to be stimulated by the addition of ATP, Mg ions and a mixture of seventeen amino acids. As in animal cells, the incorporation is inhibited by ribonuclease and the addition of RNA induces a recovery of the activity. Restoration of glutamate incorporation in the ribonuclease-treated particles could be obtained by the addition of RNA extracted from peas. Addition of RNA prepared from several sources produces a definite stimulation of the incorporation process in the intact particles. The stimulating effect of RNA is thus *not specific* and it

References p. 50/54

can still be obtained when RNA has been partially degraded during its isolation (Fig. 10). In a more recent report, Webster (1956) claims to have obtained a *net synthesis* of proteins and RNA in the particles isolated from pea roots. This synthesis requires the presence of the four nucleotides of RNA in the triphosphate form (*i.e.* adenosine, guanosine, cytidine and uridine triphosphates), of seventeen amino acids and of Mg and K ions. The inhibitors of protein synthesis are said to inhibit the concomitant RNA synthesis and the converse is also true.

Another case where ribonuclease has been found to exert marked inhibitory effects on protein synthesis is that of the *in vitro* synthesis of amylase, which was studied by Straub *et al.* (1955, 1957).

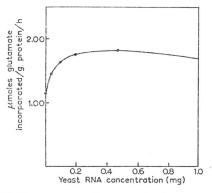

Fig. 10. Effect of RNA on glutamate incorporation in a particulate fraction of pea roots (Webster and Johnson, 1955).

This synthesis apparently occurs preferentially in the mitochondria. Nevertheless, it is strongly inhibited by the addition of ribonuclease.

While there is obviously a good deal of evidence in favor of the opinion that cytoplasmic particles, and microsomes in particular, are the major site of protein synthesis in the cell, it would, however, be an exaggeration to believe that they are the *only* site of protein synthesis. In experiments by Szafarz (1952), it appears that, when the flagellate *Polytomella* is grown in continuous culture so that all cell constituents grow at the same rate, the protein turnover is identical in all types of granules. Therefore, in the case of microorganisms kept continuously in the exponential phase of growth, microsomes cannot be the only source of cytoplasmic proteins.

Comparable observations have been made, with liver, by Khesin and Petrashkaïte (1955). They claim that, as in Webster's (1956) case, isolated cytoplasmic granules are capable of net protein synthesis. But, while in adult animals mitochondria show the same activity as microsomes, the former are said to be more active than the latter when homogenates from livers of young organisms are considered. Here again, it seems that microsomes are not the only source of cytoplasmic proteins.

Such a conclusion is in agreement with the fact reported earlier that in leaves microsomes are no more active than chloroplasts in incorporating amino acids into proteins (Stephenson and Zamecnik, 1956). Similar observations have also been made with muscle where, according to McLean et al. (1956), microsomes and mitochondria are of equal importance for protein synthesis.

In fact, more recent work by McLean et al. (1958) shows that incorporation of amino acids into mitochondria is stimulated rather than inhibited by ribonuclease. They also claim that these mitochondria are even capable of a net synthesis of cytochrome C.

There is thus no doubt that the microsomes, especially the small RNA-rich granules which they contain, play an essential part in protein synthesis. However, it would be a mistake to believe that they are the only possible site of cytoplasmic protein synthesis.

5. THE ROLE OF RNA IN PLANT VIRUSES

All the plant viruses which have been purified and in many instances crystallized, contain large amounts of RNA, ranging from 6% (tobacco mosaic virus) up to 35% (turnip yellow mosaic virus). RNA in plant viruses stands in close association with a simple protein, which is devoid of enzymatic activity.

The fact that such simple nucleoproteins are able to reproduce themselves and are thus endowed with genetic continuity is of the utmost importance. Plant viruses are ideal material for the study of the synthesis of specific proteins as well as for the solution of fundamental genetic problems. In recent years, important evidence about the respective role of RNA and proteins in plant virus multiplication has been discovered. This evidence will now be reviewed.

In their important studies on turnip yellow mosaic virus, Markham and Smith (1949) were able to separate by ultracentrifugation two distinct components from crystalline preparations of the virus. Both contained serologically identical proteins, but only the more rapidly sedimenting component also contained RNA and proved infective. This finding led Markham (1953) to the important conclusion that "there is some evidence that the nucleic acid is in fact the substance controlling virus multiplication". Markham and Smith's (1949) findings were soon extended. In 1952, Takahashi and Ishii (1952, 1953) reported the isolation from mosaic-diseased tobacco leaves of an abnormal protein which could be obtained by electrophoresis and which behaved in many ways like tobacco mosaic virus. Simultaneously, Jeener and Lemoine (1953) and Jeener et al. (1954) discovered a similar (or identical) protein and carried the matter a step further by crystallizing it. This crystallizable protein behaves in the same way as does Markham and Smith's (1949) material, i.e., it is immunologically identical with the virus, it is non-infective and it is free of RNA.

Whether these abnormal proteins present in virus-infected plants are virus precursors, intermediary stages in virus production, or by-products of the virus is still undecided. The main point is that in contrast with the complete virus they contain no RNA and are never infective.

Recent work on the structure of plant viruses (especially tobacco mosaic virus) by crystallographic and electron microscopy methods (Crick and Watson, 1956; Hart, 1955; Schramm and Zillig, 1955; Zillig et al., 1955; Fraenkel-Conrat and Williams, 1955) has considerably clarified the relationships existing between RNA and protein. Observations made by Schramm and Zillig (1955) on tobacco mosaic virus treated with sodium hydroxide have shown that the protein of the virus has a molecular weight of 17,000; on reacidification, rods having a molecular weight of 100,000 are reconstituted. But the interesting point is that an empty hole is present in the protein units or aggregates. It looks as if the RNA, which dissolves in sodium hydroxide, occupies the center of the virus particle. The correctness of this view is shown in the beautiful electron microscope photographs of Hart (1955) and Fraenkel-Conrat and Williams (1955). If the virus is treated with a detergent, filaments can be seen to project from the remains of the virus particles; these filaments disappear after treatment with ribonuclease. The protein has the structure of a pearl, in which a hole is bored for the filamentous RNA. There is no doubt that RNA, which forms a single strand, occupies the center of the particle and that it is surrounded by a protein shell.

The fact that the protein part of the virus is non-infectious, in contrast to the whole virus, suggests that RNA is really essential for the synthesis of plant viruses. If so, one could expect an inhibition of virus multiplication on the addition of substances which interfere with RNA synthesis. That this is the case has been shown conclusively by Commoner and Mercer (1952), who obtained complete inhibition of synthesis of tobacco mosaic virus by thiouracil at a concentration of $4.3 \cdot 10^{-5}$ M. This inhibition was partially reversed when uracil was added in concentrations of the same order of magnitude.

These findings of Commoner and Mercer (1952) have been confirmed by Jeener and Rosseels (1953), who obtained in addition some quite unexpected results. They found that the inhibition of virus synthesis is greater, the smaller the amount of virus present in the leaves to which thiouracil is added. This observation cannot be explained on the basis of a competition between thiouracil and uracil in some enzymatic reaction during the synthesis of RNA. It tends rather to indicate that thiouracil can be incorporated into the virus RNA and that this incorporation hinders the further multiplication of the modified particles. This interpretation of the facts has been confirmed by experiments in which ^{35}S-labeled thiouracil was added to leaves infected 2 days earlier. The concentration of thiouracil was such that the speed of virus multiplication was reduced by 50%. When the virus was collected and repeatedly crystallized, it was found that it had incorporated the labeled thiouracil in its RNA moiety only, apparently in the form of thiouridylic acid (Jeener, 1957). The correctness of these findings has been confirmed by Matthews (1956) and by Mandel *et al.* (1957). Very similar findings have been reported by Matthews (1954) in the case of 8-azaguanine. It is perfectly clear from all these experiments that the infectivity of tobacco mosaic virus is closely linked with the integrity of its RNA component. Alterations of the latter by the introduction of abnormal bases in its molecule lead to the loss of infective power, *i.e.* the nucleoprotein particle cannot be synthesized any more.

Since the presence of normal RNA is required, in addition to the presence of the non-infectious protein, to endow the tobacco mosaic virus with the capacity of synthesis, one might hope that by mixing the RNA and protein constituents partial resynthesis of the virulent particle might be achieved. Remarkable success came when Fraenkel-Conrat and Williams (1955) separated the virus protein by a sodium hydroxide treatment, and the virus RNA with a detergent. Neither of these two components was infectious as such; but on mixing together the RNA and the protein components obtained by this method, active, infectious particles could be reconstituted. Tobacco mosaic virus "resynthesized" from its RNA and protein constituents shows the typical rod-like appearance under the electron microscope. In order to obtain successful results, the tobacco mosaic virus RNA must be isolated in its native form. It loses its activity on treatment with ribonuclease and it cannot be replaced by RNA of turnip mosaic virus or by DNA. Synthetic polymers of nucleotides, prepared according to the method of Grunberg-Manago *et al.* (1956), when added to the virus protein, can reconstitute rods; but the latter are not virulent (Hart and Smith, 1956).

Considered together, all these experiments demonstrate that the RNA molecule must remain intact for virus synthesis. But, although we know that the protein part alone is non-infectious, the experiments do not prove that RNA *alone* is responsible for virus multiplication. Such a proof has been adduced by a most remarkable experiment of Gierer and Schramm (1956). By isolating tobacco mosaic virus RNA by a very mild procedure (treatment with phenol), they found that *pure virus RNA is infectious*. The purified active RNA is quickly inactivated by ribonuclease and it soon loses activity on standing, as a result of progressive denaturation. Proteolytic enzymes have no effect on the infectivity and no proteins could be detected by sensitive tests.

When Gierer and Schramm's (1956) RNA gets into tobacco leaves, it not only reproduces itself but it also synthesizes its protein counterpart and produces virus of the strain from which it originates. These experimental results are of far-reaching importance. Not only do they demonstrate the essential role of RNA in protein synthesis, but they also prove the genetic importance of RNA. In plant viruses, as pointed out by Rich and Watson (1954), Jeener (1956) and Gierer and Schramm (1956), RNA is the genetic determinant just as DNA is in phages and in cells.

It is a well-known fact that several "mutant" strains of tobacco mosaic virus exist. According to analyses by Black and Knight (1953), these strains differ in their amino acid composition rather than in their content of purine and pyrimidine bases. More recent work by Knight (1955) confirms that various strains of tobacco mosaic virus are different in their terminal amino acid residues. On the other hand, Price (1954) claims to have detected differences in the composition of the RNA part of plant virus strains. In view of these discrepancies and of the probable role of RNA as the genetic determinant in tobacco mosaic virus, crucial experiments become important. Such experiments have been made recently by Fraenkel-Conrat (1956), who brilliantly succeeded in solving the problem. Fraenkel-Conrat (1956) used the method outlined above and separated the RNA and the protein parts of different strains of tobacco mosaic virus. He then recombined the RNA from a given strain with the protein of another and succeeded in producing experimental "hybrids" between the two strains. When the virus recovered from the leaves which had been infected with these "hybrid" virus particles, it was found that the lesions produced belonged to the strain from which the RNA had been isolated. Of

References p. 50/54

still greater importance is the fact that the progeny of the hybrid virus contains both the RNA and the protein of the strain from which the RNA originates. It is therefore the RNA which carries the genetic message and which determines the specificity of the protein which has been synthesized during virus multiplication.

Finally, Schuster and Schramm (1958) recently succeeded in obtaining mutations of tobacco mosaic virus by treating the isolated RNA with nitrous acid, in order to block the amino groups of the nitrogenous bases present in RNA. They found that the alteration of a single base out of 3,300 nucleotides is enough to induce a mutation of the virus. No clearer proof that RNA really is the genetic determinant of the virus could be imagined.

6. EVIDENCE FOR THE INTERVENTION OF RNA IN PROTEIN SYNTHESIS IN LIVING CELLS

We have seen that in certain microsomal systems the destruction of RNA by ribonuclease treatment leads to a strong inhibition of the amino acid incorporation into proteins (Allfrey et al., 1953; Zamecnik and Keller, 1954; Webster and Johnson, 1955; Straub et al., 1955). Such findings provide *direct* evidence of the intervention of RNA in protein synthesis, especially when, as in Webster and Johnson's (1955) pea root system, resumption of the incorporation ability is obtained by the addition of RNA.

Similar observations have been made by Gale and Folkes (1954, 1955a) (see also reviews by Gale, 1956a, b), who studied protein metabolism in staphylococci which had been disrupted by ultrasonics. The permeability of the disrupted cells, which retain a large proportion of their nucleic acid complement, is considerably increased. Although they show no respiration, they are still capable of amino acid incorporation into proteins, and even of net protein and RNA synthesis, provided that energy sources (ATP and hexose diphosphate) as well as a mixture of amino acids are present in the medium. Removal of nucleic acids by various treatments, including digestion with specific nucleases, greatly inhibits protein synthesis. Addition of a mixture of DNA and RNA, prepared from the staphylococci themselves, largely restores the activity of the system.

Another important observation of Gale and Folkes (1954, 1955a) is that the addition of a mixture of purines and pyrimidines stimulates the induced synthesis of glucozymase in their disrupted staphylococci system, provided that amino acids are also present. After the disrupted cells have been depleted of their nucleic acids, addition of staphylococcal nucleic acids stimulates the induced enzyme synthesis. RNA is more effective for catalase synthesis than DNA, while the latter is required to restore β-galactosidase synthesis.

The experimental results, as pointed out by Gale and Folkes (1954), can be accounted for by the following hypothesis: DNA, perhaps associated with a protein, is an initial organizing structure. It is incapable of synthesizing protein itself, but it acts as an organizer for the synthesis of RNA. Once RNA has been synthesized, protein synthesis can take place at a rate dependent upon the amount of the specific RNA present.

More recently, Gale and Folkes (1955b) and Gale (1956a, b) have reported on important developments of this work. While unspecific RNA from yeast or liver is unable to restore the incorporation of amino acids into the proteins, ribonuclease digests of these ribonucleic acids are active. In the case of the staphylococcal nucleic acids, DNA loses some of its activity on digestion. In contrast, the stimulating activity of staphylococcal RNA is enhanced after the digestion. These observations led Gale and Folkes (1955b) to an extensive fractionation of staphylococcal RNA digests by chromatography and ionophoresis. Various fractions could be isolated, which promoted the incorporation of the various amino acids to different extents. Some of the fractions obtained were at least 100 times more active than the initial RNA. Gale's conclusion was (1956 b) "that the whole RNA complex is not necessary for the incorporation of any particular amino acid and that RNA can be replaced by small fragments obtained by ribonuclease digestion of the whole RNA structure".

Gale's (1956 a, b) efforts to purify the active fraction present in the ribonuclease digest have recently been concentrated on the factor which promotes the incorporation of glycine (GIF). Unfortunately, it has been impossible so far to establish its chemical nature.

Some of Gale and Folkes' (1954, 1955a) results have been quickly confirmed on a different system, the so-called *protoplasts*. These are bacteria (*Micrococcus lysodeikticus*, *B. megatherium*, etc.) which have been treated with lysozyme in sucrose solutions. The bacterial outer membrane is dissolved by such a treatment, but the rest of the protoplasm remains intact. Protoplasts constitute a very favorable system, which can be resolved by treating them with ribonuclease. Treatment of protoplasts with ribonuclease strongly inhibits the incorporation of amino acids into the proteins, while deoxyribonuclease stimulates this process (Lester, 1953; Beljanski, 1954). The ribonuclease treatment has no effect on the respiration of the protoplasts, according to Beljanski (1954).

But the most interesting results obtained so far on protoplasts are probably those of Landman and Spiegelman (1955) and of Spiegelman (1956). Protoplasts, if suitably isolated, are still capable of induced enzyme synthesis, as shown also by Wiame *et al.* (1955). β-Galactosidase synthesis was induced by Landman and Spiegelman (1955) with *B. megatherium* protoplasts; hexose diphosphate was added as an energy source and amino acids were present. This *specific* enzyme induction is almost completely inhibited by ribonuclease (1 mg/ml), which removes 80–90 % of the protoplasts' RNA. In contrast, deoxyribonuclease has a stimulating effect on the synthesis of β-galactosidase. Even when 20–25 % of the DNA has been removed from the protoplasts by deoxyribonuclease treatment, induced enzyme synthesis proceeds normally. The experiments clearly show that the integrity of RNA is more important than that of DNA for protein synthesis.

These observations raise a new and important question for the cell physiologist: is it possible to inhibit growth and protein synthesis in *living* cells or organisms by an appropriate ribonuclease treatment?

This problem has been extensively studied in the author's laboratory during the past few years. Starting from observations by Lansing and Rosenthal (1952), who found that ribonuclease treat-

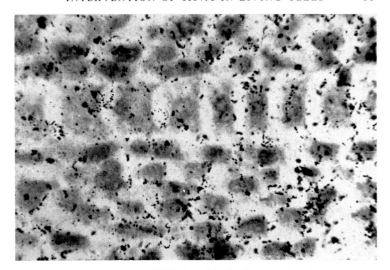

Fig. 11. Incorporation of ¹⁴C-phenylalanine in normal onion roots
(Brachet, 1954).

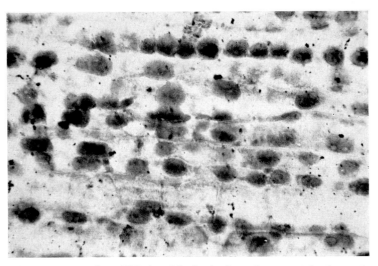

Fig. 12. Incorporation of ¹⁴C-phenylalanine in ribonuclease-treated onion roots
(Brachet, 1954).

References p. 50/54

ment decreases the basophilia of sea urchin eggs, and from the discovery by Kaufmann and Das (1955) and by Ledoux and Baltus (1954) that ribonuclease induces mitotic abnormalities in onion roots and in ascites tumor cells, we decided to study the biochemical effects of ribonuclease on various cells. The main results are summarized below.

In onion root-tips (Brachet, 1954, 1955b, 1956a), crystalline ribonuclease at 1 mg/ml concentration produces a 50% inhibition of amino acid incorporation into the proteins within 1 hour; the inhibition becomes almost complete (90%) after a 3-h treatment.

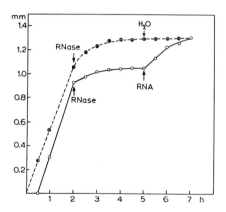

Fig. 13. Effects of ribonuclease and RNA on growth rate of onion roots. RNase: addition of Armour ribonuclease 1 mg/ml; H₂O: washed with distilled water; RNA: addition of ribonucleic acid (1%). Experiments were performed on the same onion cut into two parts. All solutions were aerated (Brachet, 1955b).

These observations were made both by conventional biochemical techniques and by autoradiography. Figs. 11 and 12 (p. 33) illustrate the type of results obtained by the autoradiography method, in the case of phenylalanine incorporation. The inhibition of the incorporation of the amino acids into proteins is faster and stronger than that of the penetration of the free amino acids. This fact indicates that the primary action of ribonuclease is less on cellular permeability than on the incorporation reaction itself.

Furthermore, ribonuclease strongly inhibits the growth of the

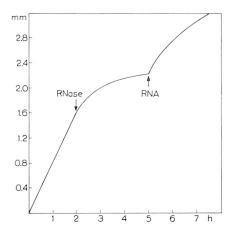

Fig. 14. Same experiment as indicated in Fig. 13, but performed on an intact onion bulb (Brachet, 1955b).

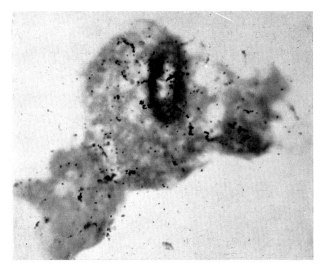

Fig. 15. Incorporation of phenylalanine into proteins of normal amoeba. Autoradiograph and Unna staining (Brachet, 1955a).

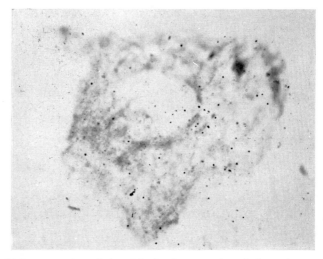

Fig. 16. Incorporation of phenylalanine into proteins of ribonuclease-treated amoeba; loss of basophilia and incorporation. Autoradiograph and Unna staining (Brachet, 1955a).

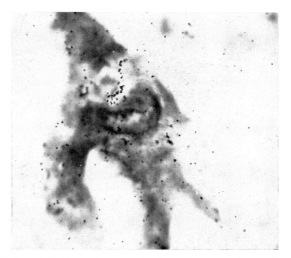

Fig. 17. Effect of addition of RNA to the ribonuclease-treated amoeba; resumption of basophilia and incorporation. Autoradiograph and Unna staining (Brachet, 1955a).

roots (Figs. 13 and 14). The effects are exactly parallel to those on the incorporation of amino acids into proteins, so that the inhibition is almost complete within 3 hours; it is usually irreversible. Chemical estimations of the protein content of the treated roots have further shown that, as might be expected, protein synthesis is almost completely inhibited.

Another interesting finding is shown in Figs. 13 and 14. The addition of yeast RNA to the treated roots partially restores growth, at least for a few hours. RNA alone exerts first a stimulation, and then an inhibition of growth in untreated roots. The results which we obtained with the living root-tip cells are thus in perfect agreement with the *in vitro* experiments of Webster and Johnson (1955) on the microsomal fraction of pea roots.

Addition of RNA can even entirely restore the incorporation of amino acids into proteins of ribonuclease-treated roots, provided that the ribonuclease treatment was such as to produce a 60–70% inhibition of the incorporation. In these experiments, RNA isolated from onion roots was about 4 times more active than yeast RNA in reactivating the protein synthesis. (Sels-Brygier, 1958).

The mode of action of ribonuclease, in the case of living onion roots, is certainly complex and is not yet completely understood. It is certain, however, that the inhibition of protein synthesis is not a result of an indirect effect of the enzyme on energy-producing reactions. The oxygen consumption remains essentially normal even after a 3-h ribonuclease treatment and the ATP level shows a slight increase. It is also unlikely that ribonuclease produces a marked breakdown of RNA in the living cells. No consistent results were obtained when the RNA content and the incorporation of precursors (^{32}P, adenine) into the RNA molecule were studied in the treated roots. Depending upon the species of onions and the ribonuclease preparations used, stimulation or inhibition of RNA synthesis and RNA metabolism were obtained. Breakdown of the RNA could, however, be obtained after longer times of action (4–6 h).

Very recently, we were able to show that ribonuclease quickly breaks down the RNA which is present in the supernatant fraction

References p. 50/54

of a homogenate of roots. The significance of this soluble RNA will be discussed later (Brachet and Six, 1959).

In conclusion, there is no doubt that ribonuclease can penetrate into onion roots, where it inhibits protein synthesis. Its mode of action is probably a dual one: it breaks down the soluble RNA and it apparently forms a complex with the RNA of the microsomes and the nucleoli. Evidence for such a complex formation is found in the fact that onion root-tip cells, as might be expected from the direct RNA estimations, do not lose their basophilia unless they have been acted upon by ribonuclease for more than 3 hours. But, if the ribonuclease-treated roots are fixed by freeze-substitution, instead of the usual Zenker acetic treatment, cytoplasmic baso-philia disappears from the outer layer after only 1 hour; nuclear basophilia is destroyed in almost all cells. After a 3-h ribonuclease treatment, basophilia (except for chromatin) practically disappears in the roots fixed by freeze substitution; on the other hand, staining remains unimpaired in the Zenker-fixed roots, which cannot be distinguished from the control roots. Obviously ribonuclease, es-pecially in the nucleoli, forms a complex with RNA. This complex remains intact in the roots fixed by freeze substitution, while it is broken down by an energetic fixative such as Zenker.

More interesting perhaps is the case of the amoeba, *Amoeba pro-teus* (Brachet, 1955a, 1956b). Very low concentrations of ribonu-clease (0.05–0.01 mg/ml) are sufficient to produce loss of locomo-tion, followed by cytolysis after 2–3 h. If the amoebae are returned to a normal medium after $1\frac{1}{2}$ h, they ultimately die, even if they are provided with food. But complete recovery of a given percentage (20–50 %) of the amoebae population is obtained if the ribonuclease-treated amoebae are placed in the same medium supplemented with yeast RNA (1.4 mg/ml). The shape, locomotion and ability to multiply (if properly fed) are almost normal in the amoebae which have recovered in this way.

Cytochemical observations indicate that, in contrast to onion root-tip cells, ribonuclease-treated amoebae lose to a considerable extent their affinity for basic dyes (Figs. 15, 16, 17, p. 35 and p. 36). Both the cytoplasm and the nucleoli show decreased basophilia, while the DNA-containing chromatin stains normally. Quantitative estimations of the RNA content confirm that a marked drop (20–45%) occurs. Simultaneously, the content of acid-soluble nucleotides increases. The RNA content of the amoebae which have been treated successively with ribonuclease and RNA is essentially normal. RNA alone produces a small but significant increase in the RNA content of normal untreated amoebae. As in the onion root-tips, the oxygen consumption of the ribonuclease-treated amoebae undergoes little change, while their ATP content increases somewhat (Skreb-Guilcher, 1955).

It is thus possible to modify almost at will the RNA content of the amoebae by suitable treatment with ribonuclease and RNA. What are the consequences of such changes on amino acid incorporation into proteins? Autoradiography experiments with ^{14}C-phenylalanine show that ribonuclease produces an almost complete (90%) inhibition of the incorporation into the proteins. When the ribonuclease-treated amoebae are placed in the normal medium enriched in RNA, basophilia, as we have seen, returns to normal in some of the amoebae. The autoradiography observations show that a limited number of these basophilic amoebae recover the capacity to incorporate phenylalanine into the proteins. (Figs. 15, 16, 17). Replacement of the specific RNA of the amoebae by unspecific yeast RNA, although it has favorable effects on the survival, the basophilia, and the motility of the ribonuclease-treated organisms, does not ensure normal protein anabolism.

In order to reach a better understanding of the mechanisms of action of ribonuclease and RNA in living amoebae, more should be known about the penetration of these substances in these organisms. Our latest observations (Brachet, 1956b, Brachet et al., 1957; Schumaker, 1958) lead to the conclusion that the penetration of ribonuclease into the amoebae is a very rapid process, probably linked to pinocytosis. In fact, pinocytosis has been found to occur even for low concentrations of ribonuclease by Chapman-Andresen and Prescott (1956). Even 5 to 15 minutes after ribonuclease has been added to the amoebae, their basophilia decreases, especially in the nucleoli and a measurable drop (10%) in the RNA content is already found. At the same time, the ribonuclease content of the amoebae increases 2–3 times. Autoradiography observations with radio-iodine-labeled ribonuclease confirm the penetration of the enzyme in the amoebae, including their nucleus.

According to the recent analysis of Schumaker (1958), ribonuclease first combines with acidic sites on the membrane; the latter, afterwards, become ingested through pinocytosis.

Once it has penetrated into the amoebae, the enzyme produces many reactions. Besides the attack on RNA, complex formation, as in onion roots, with RNA is a possibility which cannot be ruled out. Substances which combine with ribonuclease without being broken down (DNA, synthetic purine polynucleotides of Grunberg-Manago *et al.*, 1955, 1956) markedly protect the amoebae against the effects of ribonuclease when both are mixed together. The addition to the ribonuclease (in the external medium) of substances which are good substrates for the enzyme, *e.g.* synthetic pyrimidine polynucleotides of Grunberg-Manago *et al.* (1955, 1956), and of mononucleotides has little protective value.

Ribonuclease also exerts a marked inhibitory effect on the digestion of the preys ingested by the amoebae. Direct estimations have shown that protease and dipeptidase activities are strongly reduced in the ribonuclease-treated amoebae. Further work is required to establish whether all enzymes or only those dealing with protein metabolism are inhibited in the ribonuclease-treated organisms (Briers *et al.*, 1957).

Despite the complexity and difficulty of interpretation of the experimental results, the essential fact is that in all the cells in which ribonuclease penetrates inhibition of protein anabolism quickly follows. For instance, in frog and starfish oöcytes (Ficq and Errera, 1955) treatment with ribonuclease produces a considerable drop in basophilia (after freeze-substitution fixation). There is a parallel inhibition of the incorporation of phenylalanine into the proteins of the RNA-rich nucleoli and cytoplasm. In this case, one is almost certainly dealing with the formation of a RNA-ribonuclease complex, as in the onion root-tips. Basophilia remains normal in Zenker fixed oöcytes and chemical methods show no actual decrease in the total RNA content. In fact, this complex breaks down spontaneously when the eggs are simply washed and left in normal sea water. After a few hours, basophilia (after freeze-substitution) and incorporation of amino acids into proteins simultaneously return to normal.

A somewhat different mode of action is found for ribonuclease in the case of ascites tumor cells (Ledoux and Baltus, 1954; Ledoux and Revell, 1955; Ledoux et al., 1956; Ledoux and Vanderhaeghe, 1956; Pileri et al., 1959). The enzyme penetrates by pinocytosis into these cells in the same way as into the amoebae; but it induces an increased synthesis of RNA as an initial stage. This newly synthesized RNA is apparently abnormal in nature, since its composition in bases differs from that of the initial RNA. As a result, incorporation of amino acids into proteins is already inhibited during this first synthetic phase. Later on, the RNA content considerably decreases and the cells finally break down. Many free nuclei are found at the time in the ascites fluid. These interesting results of Ledoux and his co-workers are of obvious importance for the chemotherapy of cancer. It is clear that if growth is linked to protein synthesis and RNA metabolism, ribonuclease would be expected to inhibit the growth of tumors, provided that the enzyme can penetrate into the cancer cells. This has frequently been found to be the case by Ledoux (1955a, b), who claims that the survival time of tumor-bearing mice is significantly increased when they are injected intraperitoneally with ribonuclease.

The strong antimitotic activity of ribonuclease, which was first discovered by Kaufmann and Das (1955) for onion root-tips, has been confirmed for amphibian eggs (Ledoux et al., 1955; Brachet and Ledoux, 1955) and for tissue cultures (Chèvremont and Chèvremont-Comhaire, 1955). The results obtained with amphibian eggs during cleavage will be discussed in the next chapter.

Ribonuclease does not, of course, penetrate into all cells (Brachet, 1955a). Algae, yeast cells, molds and ciliates are usually insensitive to its action, probably because of lack of penetration through thick membranes or rigid cortex, and the absence of pinocytosis. The situation is more complex in the case of bacteria. In B. megatherium,

References p. 50/54

according to Groth (1956), ribonuclease strongly inhibits growth and amino acid incorporation into the bacterial proteins; simultaneously, the RNA content of the treated bacteria decreases significantly. A detailed reinvestigation of the same problem by Jeener (1959) shows that the situation is very complex in the case of both lysogenic and normal bacteria. Among the latter, different mutant strains, distinguishable by their sensitivity to different concentrations of ribonuclease, have been detected and isolated. As in onion root-tips, ribonuclease does not necessarily break down the RNA. Whenever the enzyme is active on a given strain, its primary effect is an antimitotic one.

There is excellent evidence also that ribonuclease strongly interferes with virus multiplication. As shown first by Kleczkowski and Kleczkowski (1954). The enzyme inhibits the multiplication of *Rhizobium* bacteriophage. The addition of the enzyme after the phage has already combined with the bacteria does not prevent the phage from multiplying, but it decreases the rate of multiplication of both the phage and the bacteria. Experiments on tobacco mosaic virus by Casterman and Jeener (1955) and by Bawden and Harrison (1955) have confirmed that ribonuclease inhibits virus synthesis. The enzyme does not act directly on the virus RNA, which is protected against the enzyme by its protein shell. If ribonuclease is injected into tobacco leaves before the virus is added, it completely prevents the infection. If, on the other hand, the enzyme is injected into already infected leaves, virus multiplication is only prevented during the first few hours after the injection (Hamers-Casterman and Jeener, 1957).

Essentially similar observations have been made on influenza (Le Clerc, 1956; Le Clerc and Brachet, 1957) and avian pest (Zillig *et al.*, 1955) viruses. In the case of influenza virus, Le Clerc's careful analysis clearly shows that ribonuclease does not act directly on the virus; nor does the enzyme inhibit amino acid incorporation in the host cells (chorio-allantoic membrane). Ribonuclease only stops the growth of the virus when it is added shortly after the infection. The general conclusion of these experiments is the same: ribonuclease inhibits multiplication of the virus when the latter is in the so-called "dark phase", *i.e.*, when no complete infectious virus particles can be recovered from the infected host cells. A very interesting hypothesis, proposed by Casterman and Jeener (1955) and by Le Clerc (1956), gives a satisfactory explanation of the present facts. Both tobacco mosaic virus and influenza virus would, immediately after infection, break down into RNA and protein. The RNA would, as already discussed earlier, play the same genetic role as DNA in phage infection. During that initial period, where RNA would be separated from the protein constituent of the virus, RNA would of course be extremely sensitive to ribonuclease. Its destruction would result in the loss of infectivity. Such an explanation is obviously in keeping with all that has been said earlier in this chapter on the genetic role of RNA in plant viruses.

But there is an alternative, perhaps more probable, explanation. On penetration of the virus, the infected host cell would build a new specific RNA. This RNA synthesis would be necessary for virus multiplication and it would be inhibited by ribonuclease. There is, in fact, good evidence for the view that in the *E. coli*-T phages system, synthesis of new RNA molecules in the bacterium immediately follows the injection of phage DNA (Volkin *et al.*, 1958). Jeener's (1959) recent experiments clearly show that, in a comparable system, ribonuclease inhibits phage multiplication, although the latter contains no RNA. It has also been reported by Tamm (1948) that ribonuclease inhibits the multiplication of another DNA-containing virus, that of vaccinia. Further experiments are obviously needed before all the facts already known about the effects of ribonuclease on virus multiplication can be adequately explained.

To summarize, ribonuclease can penetrate into a number of cells and organisms. The enzyme does not interfere with the energy-producing mechanisms and it has complex effects on RNA metabolism. Enzyme-substrate complex formation is usually followed, sooner or later, by an enzymatic breakdown of the RNA. In all cases studied so far, incorporation of amino acids into proteins, protein synthesis, mitotic activity and growth have been drastically inhibited. Addition of foreign RNA, in many instances, exerts favorable effects on the ribonuclease-treated cells. The experiments

References p. 50/54

strongly indicate that, in living cells, RNA integrity is essential for protein synthesis. The probable biochemical mechanisms of the latter will now be studied briefly.

7. BIOCHEMICAL MECHANISMS OF PROTEIN SYNTHESIS

A number of substances are required for protein synthesis. The presence of an amino acid pool is obviously necessary and it is clear from the foregoing that ATP, a soluble enzyme fraction and RNA are all indispensable for amino acid incorporation into the proteins of relatively simple systems, isolated microsomes, for instance. In the following discussion the theory which is now generally accepted and which involves all these substances (amino acids, ATP, soluble enzymes and RNA) will be briefly presented. We shall first consider the role of ATP and the soluble enzymes, and then that of RNA.

a. ATP and the soluble enzymes fraction of Hoagland

The necessity of an energy supply for peptide synthesis has been repeatedly emphasized by Borsook (1950, 1953, 1956a, b), Lipmann (1949), Chantrenne (1951) and others. Borsook's (1950) experiments have conclusively demonstrated that incorporation of labeled amino acids into proteins requires energy. The process is stopped, or markedly reduced, by anaerobiosis or addition of cyanide, azide dinitrophenol, etc. In the homogenate system of Siekevitz (1952) this uptake of tagged amino acids into proteins is more closely linked to phosphorylation than to oxidation. The evidence for the necessity of ATP as an energy source in amino acid incorporation into proteins is still stronger in the experiments performed by Zamecnik and Keller (1954) with isolated microsomes. As we have seen, incorporation proceeds provided that microsomes, a non-dialyzable soluble fraction and an ATP-generating system are present. This system is mainly localized in the mitochondria in the normal living cell. The mitochondria therefore probably play an important part in protein synthesis. But it is an indirect one, for their main function is to generate the energy-rich bonds of ATP. In the simplified homogenate systems mitochondria can be dispensed with provided that ATP is produced or present. As a matter of fact, the mere presence of ATP (and guanosine diphosphate (GDP) or guanosine triphosphate (GTP), which probably play a similar role, according to Littlefield *et al.*, 1955, and Keller and Zamecnik, 1956) is enough to obtain full incorporation activity with the small granules of ascites tumor cells, in the presence of the soluble factor. This is due to the fact that these small granules have little or no adenosine triphosphatase activity, so that ATP is entirely available for the incorporation reaction. Addition of enzymatic systems which utilize ATP, and therefore compete with the microsomes for ATP in the homogenates, results in a décrease in the incorporation of the amino acids into the proteins (Siekevitz, 1952; Titova and Shapot, 1955). Conversely, the ATP content of the cells increases somewhat when protein synthesis is inhibited. This is the case, as we have seen, for onion roots (Brachet, 1954) or amoebae (Skreb-Guilcher, 1955) treated with ribonuclease. The same is also true for enucleate fragments of amoebae (Brachet, 1955a). This increase in the ATP content of the cells in which protein anabolism is restricted is apparently a consequence of the unemployment of the high energy phosphate bonds.

Recent work by Hoagland (1955) and by De Moss and Novelli (1955) has shown that a soluble, non-dialyzable factor is required for the incorporation of amino acids into proteins, besides ATP and RNA. According to Hoagland (1955), this soluble fraction contains enzymes which catalyze the exchange of radioactive pyrophosphate and ATP. Addition of an amino acid, or better, a mixture of amino acids, increases the speed of the exchange reaction two to three times. The following scheme has been proposed by Hoagland (1955) in order to explain the activation of amino acids (AA):

1. E_1 ⌐¯¯¬ + ATP = E_1 ⌐AMP — PP⌐

in which E_1 is the activation site of the amino acid on the enzyme. It would bind ATP in such a way as to make the AMP —PP bond more labile.

References p. 50/54

2. $E_1 \rfloor \text{AMP} - \text{PP} \lfloor + \text{AA} = E_1 \rfloor \text{AMP} - \text{AA} \lfloor + \text{PP}$

$$\underset{\substack{\text{activated amino} \\ \text{acid}}}{} \qquad \underset{\text{pyrophosphate}}{}$$

The activated amino acid can then react with hydroxylamine according to the reaction:

3. $E_1 \rfloor \text{AMP} - \text{AA} \lfloor + \text{NH}_2\text{OH} = E_1 + \text{AA} - \text{NH}_2\text{OH} + \text{AMP}$

Under physiological conditions, hydroxylamine would be replaced by an amino acid or a peptide bound to the microsomes.

Later work by De Moss et al. (1956) has given some indication about the biochemical mechanism of Hoagland's (1955) reaction. In the case of the amino acid leucine, a leucyl-AMP compound acts as the intermediate promoting the exchange reaction between ATP and pyrophosphate, since synthetic leucyl-AMP is active in the absence of the enzyme. Amino acid-AMP compounds thus represent the activated amino acids, which will ultimately become part of the protein.

Hoagland et al. (1956) also obtained definite evidence showing that their soluble enzyme really activates the carboxyl group of the amino acids.

More recent work has shown that the amino acid becomes attached to the ribose moiety of adenylic acid. It has also been shown clearly that there are many distinct activating enzymes— possibly one for each of the amino acids. One of them, the enzyme which activates tryptophane, has even been crystallized.

b. The role of RNA in protein synthesis

In a very important paper, Hoagland et al. (1957) have shown that the incorporation of amino acids into proteins occurs in three successive steps. After the formation of the amino acyl-AMP compound, the activated amino acid is transferred to the RNA present in the soluble fraction. This second step is very sensitive to ribonuclease. Guanosine triphosphate finally acts as an intermediate in the transfer of this activated amino acid to a peptide linkage, via the microsomes, by a mechanism which is as yet unknown.

The existence of a transfer of the activated amino acid to soluble

RNA has been repeatedly confirmed since Hoagland *et al.*'s (1957) initial observations. There is growing evidence for the view that this soluble fraction is, in fact, a mixture of many different specific RNA's. Each of them would be a specific acceptor for a definite amino acid.

The role of soluble RNA in protein synthesis and the great sensitivity of the reaction to ribonuclease offer an explanation of the results presented in section 6 (p. 30) on the effects of this enzyme on living cells. As already pointed out, in onion roots at least, treatment of the living cells with ribonuclease leads to a rapid and considerable (50%) decrease in the soluble RNA content, without affecting the RNA present in cell particles (Brachet and Six, 1959). It would certainly be interesting to extend these observations to other cells in which ribonuclease stops protein synthesis *in vitro*.

The mechanism of protein synthesis in three different steps (activation of the amino acid by ATP and the soluble enzymes, incorporation of the amino acid into soluble RNA, and incorporation of the latter into microsomal RNA) which has been postulated by Hoagland *et al.* (1957) is certainly basically correct. But, for the biologist, and especially for the geneticist and the immunologist, the major problem to be solved is the mechanism of *specific* protein synthesis. This problem is still at the stage of ingenious hypotheses. The major one, for which there is no satisfactory substitute so far, is the so-called *template* hypothesis, which postulates the existence of a model (template) under the influence of which the building blocks (the amino acids) are arranged in the right order. The template would act as a mold forming a counterpart to the protein to be formed. It is tempting to suppose, as many have already done (Friedrich-Freksa, 1940; Rondoni, 1940; Haurowitz, 1949, 1952 and Caldwell and Hinshelwood, 1950), that it is RNA which represents the counterpart to the protein. More recently, this view has also been accepted by Borsook (1956a,b) and an impressive case has been made in its favor by Spiegelman *et al.* (1955) and by Spiegelman (1956).

The main argument in favor of the template theory is the fact that in many instances protein synthesis occurs directly at the expense of free amino acids, without the formation of peptides as intermediates. The fact is now well established in the case of induced enzyme synthesis in microörganisms, as well as in the tissues of higher organisms.

While there is no evidence to prove conclusively that RNA is the template, many experimental results fit in well with this hypothesis. For instance, it has been demonstrated that in pancreatic tissue which has been stimulated to enzyme production by pilocarpine (Hokin, 1952; De Deken-Grenson, 1953a, b) and in the secreting oviduct of laying hens (Grenson, 1952), the synthesis of proteins is not linked to the rate of uptake of ^{32}P by RNA. These observations are in better agreement with the template hypothesis than with any other. As Hokin (1952) points out, it would seem that RNA plays a part during the rearrangement and movement of enzymes during secretion. Nucleoproteins or RNA might act as a specific framework on to which enzyme systems could be organized and which could direct the synthesis of more RNA. Such a view is consistent with the results of Daly and Mirsky (1952) which indicate that the total protein content of the pancreas remains constant during the cycle of secretion and synthesis. When enzyme secretion takes place, rapid synthesis of a precursor protein would occur and this would be followed by gradual transformation into the characteristic pancreatic enzymes.

Some evidence for the template theory has been introduced by Gale and Folkes (1955b). They also showed that in their above-mentioned experiments with disrupted staphylococci, RNA could be replaced by small fragments obtained by ribonuclease digestion of the whole RNA molecule. As pointed out by Gale (1956a, b), these results might be explained on the assumption that "complete nucleic acid may present a linked series of specific loci each of which corresponds to the position of a specific amino acid in a protein sequence. The promotion of incorporation by exchange would thus depend upon the order of the loci in a particular nucleic acid, and the species specificity of undigested nucleic acids in this respect would be explained."

Still another observation, which agrees well with the template hypothesis, is that of Chargaff *et al.* (1956). They analyzed the chemical composition of the small ribonucleoprotein granules which were isolated from microsomes after deoxycholate treatment and ultracentrifugation, according to Littlefield *et al.* (1955). In agreement with the template theory, they found two amino acid residues for one nucleotide residue, and further showed that all of the protein is linked to RNA in these small particles.

Also in favor of the template hypothesis is the fact, reported by Potter and Dounce (1956a, b), that alkaline digests of RNA from various sources (yeast, mammalian tissues) contain amino acids or small peptides attached to nucleotides. The amino acids and the nucleotides might possibly be bound together by phospho-amide linkages.

Finally, it seems impossible to explain the recent findings made in the field on tobacco mosaic virus reproduction by any theory simpler than that of the template. In tobacco mosaic virus, RNA acts as a specific model which determines the structure of the protein which is synthesized (Jeener, 1956; Fraenkel-Conrat, 1956; Gierer and Schramm, 1956 and others).

It will be an important task for the future to explain how RNA might act in a template mechanism. At present, we have only clever theories and hypotheses. Unfortunately, they are still based on so little experimental evidence that it would be fruitless to go into them here.

REFERENCES

ABOLINS, L., (1952) *Exptl. Cell Research*, 3, 1.
ALLFREY, V. G., M. M. DALY AND A. E. MIRSKY, (1953) *J. Gen. Physiol.*, 37, 157.
ALLFREY, V. G., M. M. DALY, A. E. MIRSKY, (1955a) *J. Gen. Physiol.*, 38, 415.
ALLFREY, V. G., A. E. MIRSKY AND S. OSAWA, (1955b) *Nature*, 176, 1042.
BAWDEN, F. C. AND B. D. HARRISON, (1955) *J. Gen. Microbiol.*, 13, 494.
BELJANSKI, M., (1954) *Biochim. Biophys. Acta*, 15, 425.
BEN-ISHAI, R. AND B. E. VOLCANI, (1956) *Biochim. Biophys. Acta*, 21, 265.
BLACK, F. L. AND C. A. KNIGHT, (1953) *J. Biol. Chem.*, 202, 51.
BORSOOK, H., (1950) *Physiol. Revs.*, 30, 206.
BORSOOK, H., (1953) *Advances in Protein Chem.*, 8, 128.
BORSOOK, H., (1956a) in: *Proceedings 3rd Intern. Congress of Biochemistry*, C. LIÉBECQ, ed. Academic Press, New York, p. 92.
BORSOOK, H., (1956b) *J. Cellular Comp. Physiol.*, 47, suppl. 1, 35.
BORSOOK, H., C. L. DEASY, A. J. HAAGEN-SMIT, G. KEIGHLEY AND P. H. LOWY, (1950) *J. Biol. Chem.*, 184, 529.
BRACHET, J., (1933) *Arch. biol. (Liège)*, 44, 519.
BRACHET, J., (1941) *Enzymologia*, 10, 87.
BRACHET, J., (1942) *Arch. biol. (Liège)*, 53, 207.
BRACHET, J., (1954) *Nature*, 174, 876.
BRACHET, J., (1955a) *Nature*, 175, 851.
BRACHET, J., (1955b) *Biochim. Biophys. Acta*, 16, 611.
BRACHET, J., (1956a) *Biochim. Biophys. Acta*, 19, 583.
BRACHET, J., (1956b) *Exptl. Cell Research*, 10, 255.
BRACHET, J., (1957) *Biochemical Cytology*, Academic Press, New York.
BRACHET, J., (1960) *The Biochemistry of Development*, Pergamon Press, London.
BRACHET, J. AND R. JEENER, (1944) *Enzymologia*, 11, 196.
BRACHET, J. AND L. LEDOUX, (1955) *Exptl. Cell Research*, suppl. 3, 27.
BRACHET, J. AND N. SIX, (1959) *Biochim. Biophys. Acta*, 35, 580.
BRACHET, J., R. JEENER, M. ROSSEEL AND L. THONET, (1946) *Bull. soc. chim. biol.*, 28, 460.
BRACHET, J., M. BRIERS AND Y. THOMAS, (1957) *Biochem. J.*, 66, 14.
BRIERS, M., Y. THOMAS AND J. BRACHET, (1957) *Arch. intern. physiol. et biochim.*, 65, 157.
CALDWELL, P. C. AND C. HINSHELWOOD, (1950) *J. Chem. Soc.*, 3156.
CALDWELL, P. C., E. L. MACKOR, C. HINSHELWOOD, (1950) *J. Chem. Soc.*, 3151.
CAMPBELL, R. M. AND H. W. KOSTERLITZ, (1952) *Biochim. Biophys. Acta*, 8, 664.
CASPERSSON, T., (1936) *Skand. Arch. Physiol.*, 73, suppl. 8.
CASPERSSON, T., (1940) *J. Roy. Microscop. Soc.*, 68, 8.
CASPERSSON, T., (1941) *Naturwissenschaften*, 29, 33.
CASPERSSON, T. AND K. BRANDT, (1941) *Protoplasma*, 35, 507.
CASPERSSON, T. AND J. SCHULTZ, (1938) *Nature*, 142, 294.
CASTERMAN, C. AND R. JEENER, (1955) *Biochim. Biophys. Acta*, 16, 433.
CHANTRENNE, H., (1951) *Pubbl. staz. zool. Napoli*, 23, suppl., 70.

CHANTRENNE, H., (1956a) Nature, 177, 579.
CHANTRENNE, H., (1956b) Arch. Biochem. Biophys., 65, 414.
CHAPMAN-ANDRESEN, C. AND D. M. PRESCOTT, (1956) Compt. rend. trav. lab. Carlsberg, Sér. chim., 30, 57.
CHARGAFF, E., D. ELSON AND T. SHIGEURA, (1956) Nature, 178, 682.
CHÈVREMONT, M. AND S. CHÈVREMONT-COMHAIRE, (1955) Nature, 176, 1075.
CLAUDE, A., (1943) Biol. Symposia, 10, 3.
COHEN, S. S. AND H. D. BARNER, (1954) Proc. Natl. Acad. Sci. U.S., 40, 885.
COHEN, S. S. AND H. D. BARNER, (1955) J. Bacteriol., 69, 59.
COMMONER, B. AND J. MERCER, (1952) Arch. Biochem. Biophys. 35, 278.
CRICK, F. H. C. AND J. D. WATSON, (1956) Nature, 177, 473.
DALY, M. M. AND A. E. MIRSKY, (1952) J. Gen. Physiol., 36, 243.
DALY, M. M., V. G. ALLFREY AND A. E. MIRSKY, (1955) J. Gen. Physiol., 39, 207.
DAVIDSON, J. N., (1947) Cold Spring Harbor Symposia Quant. Biol., 12, 50.
DAVIDSON, J. N., (1953) The Biochemistry of Nucleic Acids, Wiley, New York.
DE DEKEN-GRENSON, M., (1953a) Biochim. Biophys. Acta, 10, 480.
DE DEKEN-GRENSON, M., (1953b) Biochim. Biophys. Acta, 12, 560.
DE MOSS, J. A. AND G. D. NOVELLI, (1955) Biochim. Biophys. Acta, 18, 592.
DE MOSS, J. A., S. M. GENUTH AND G. D. NOVELLI, (1956) Proc. Natl. Acad. Sci. U.S., 42, 325.
DENUCÉ, J. M., (1952) Biochim. Biophys. Acta, 8, 3.
DESCLIN, L., (1940) Compt. rend. soc. biol., 133, 457.
DI STEFANO, H. S., A. D. BASS, H. F. DIERMEYER AND J. TEPPERMAN, (1952) Endocrinology, 51, 386.
DI STEFANO, H. S., H. F. DIERMEYER AND J. TEPPERMAN, (1955) Endocrinology, 57, 158.
FEULGEN, R. AND H. ROSSENBECK, (1924) Z. physiol. Chem. Hoppe-Seyler's, 135, 203.
FIALA, S., E. E. SPROUL AND A. E. FIALA, (1956) Federation Proc., 15, 515.
FICQ, A., (1955) Exptl. Cell Research, 9, 286.
FICQ, A. AND J. BRACHET, (1956) Exptl. Cell Research, 11, 146.
FICQ, A. AND M. ERRERA, (1955) Arch. intern. physiol. et biochim., 63, 259.
FRAENKEL-CONRAT, H., (1956) J. Am. Chem. Soc., 78, 882.
FRAENKEL-CONRAT, H. AND R. C. WILLIAMS, (1955) Proc. Natl. Acad. Sci. U.S., 41, 690.
FRIEDRICH-FREKSA, H., (1940) Naturwissenschaften, 28, 376.
GALE, E. F., (1956a) in: Ciba Foundation Symposium on Ionising Radiations and Cell Metabolism, Churchill, London, p. 147.
GALE, E. F., (1956b) in: Proceedings 3rd Intern. Congress of Biochemistry, C. LIÉBECQ, ed., Academic Press, New York, p. 345.
GALE, E. F. AND J. P. FOLKES, (1953) Biochem. J., 55, 721, 730.
GALE, E. F. AND J. P. FOLKES, (1954) Nature, 172, 1223.
GALE, E. F. AND J. P. FOLKES, (1955a) Biochem. J., 59, 661, 675.
GALE, E. F. AND J. P. FOLKES, (1955b) Nature, 175, 592.
GAVOSTO, F. AND R. RECHENMANN, (1954) Biochim. Biophys. Acta, 13, 583.
GIERER, A. AND G. SCHRAMM, (1956) Z. Naturforsch., 11b, 138.

GORDON, M. W. AND J. I. NURNBERGER, (1955) *Exptl. Cell Research*, *8*, 279.
GRENSON, M., (1952) *Biochim. Biophys. Acta*, *9*, 102.
GROTH, D. P., (1956) *Biochim. Biophys. Acta*, *21*, 18.
GRUNBERG-MANAGO, M., P. J. ORTIZ AND S. OCHOA, (1955) *Science*, *122*, 907.
GRUNBERG-MANAGO, M., P. J. ORTIZ AND S. OCHOA, (1956) *Biochim. Biophys. Acta*, *20*, 285.
HAGUENAU, F., (1958) *Intern. Rev. Cytol.*, *7*, 425.
HALVORSON, H. O. AND L. JACKSON, (1956) *J. Gen. Microbiol.*, *14*, 26.
HAMERS-CASTERMAN, C. AND R. JEENER, (1957) *Virology*, *3*, 197.
HART, R. C., (1955) *Proc. Natl. Acad. Sci. U.S.*, *41*, 261.
HART, R. C. AND J. D. SMITH, (1956) *Nature*, *178*, 739.
HAUROWITZ, F., (1949) *Quart. Rev. Biol.*, *24*, 93.
HAUROWITZ, F., (1952) *Biol. Revs. Cambridge Phil. Soc.*, *27*, 247.
HENDLER, R. W., (1959) *J. biol. Chem.*, *234*, 1466.
HERLANT, M., (1943) *Arch. biol. (Liège)*, *54*, 225.
HOAGLAND, M. B., (1955) *Biochim. Biophys. Acta*, *16*, 288.
HOAGLAND, M. B., P. C. ZAMECNIK AND M. L. STEPHENSON, (1956) *J. Biol. Chem.*, *218*, 345.
HOAGLAND, M. B., P. C. ZAMECNIK AND M. L. STEPHENSON, (1957) *Biochim. Biophys. Acta*, *24*, 215.
HOKIN, L. E., (1952) *Biochim. Biophys. Acta*, *8*, 225.
HULTIN, T., (1950) *Exptl. Cell Research*, *1*, 376, 599.
JEENER, H. AND R. JEENER, (1952) *Exptl. Cell Research*, *3*, 675.
JEENER, R., (1952) *Biochim. Biophys. Acta*, *8*, 125.
JEENER, R., (1953) *Arch. Biochem. Biophys.*, *43*, 381.
JEENER, R., (1956) *Advances in Enzymol.*, *17*, 477.
JEENER, R., (1957) *Biochim. Biophys. Acta*, *23*, 351.
JEENER, R., (1959) *Biochim. Biophys. Acta*, *32*, 106.
JEENER, R. AND P. LEMOINE, (1953) *Nature*, *171*, 935.
JEENER, R. AND J. ROSSEELS, (1953) *Biochim. Biophys. Acta*, *11*, 438.
JEENER, R., P. LEMOINE AND C. LAVAND'HOMME, (1954) *Biochim. Biophys. Acta*, *14*, 321.
JENSEN, W. A., (1955) *Exptl. Cell Research*, *10*, 222.
KANAZIR, D. AND M. ERRERA, (1954) *Biochim. Biophys. Acta*, *14*, 62.
KAUFMANN, B. P. AND N. K. DAS, (1955) *Chromosoma*, *7*, 19.
KELLER, E. B., (1951) *Federation Proc.*, *10*, 106.
KELLER, E. B. AND P. C. ZAMECNIK, (1956) *J. Biol. Chem.*, *221*, 43.
KELNER, A., (1953) *J. Bacteriol.*, *65*, 252.
KHESIN, R. V. AND S. K. PETRASHKAĬTE, (1955) *Biokhimiya*, *20*, 597.
KLECZKOWSKI, J. AND A. KLECZKOWSKI, (1954) *J. Gen. Microbiol.*, *11*, 451.
KNIGHT, C. A., (1955) *J. Biol. Chem.*, *214*, 231.
KONING, A. L. AND H. C. HAMILTON, (1954) *J. Gen. Microbiol.*, *11*, 451.
KURNICK, E., (1955) *J. Histochem. and Cytochem.*, *3*, 290.
LAIRD, A. K., A. D. BARTON AND O. NYGAARD, (1955) *Exptl. Cell Research*, *9*, 523.
LANDMAN, O. E. AND S. SPIEGELMAN, (1955) *Proc. Natl. Acad. Sci. U.S.*, *41*, 698.
LANSING, A. AND T. B. ROSENTHAL, (1952) *J. Cellular Comp. Physiol.*, *40*, 337.

Le Clerc, J., (1956) *Nature, 177*, 578.
Le Clerc, J. and J. Brachet, (1957) *Semaine hôp., N° 12*, 1361.
Ledoux, L., (1955a) *Nature, 175*, 258.
Ledoux, L., (1955b) *Nature, 176*, 36.
Ledoux, L. and E. Baltus, (1954) *Experientia, 10*, 501.
Ledoux, L. and S. H. Revell, (1955) *Biochim. Biophys. Acta, 18*, 416.
Ledoux, L. and F. Vanderhaeghe, (1956) *Arch. intern. physiol. et biochim., 64*, 537.
Ledoux, L., E. Baltus and F. Vanderhaeghe, (1956) *Arch. intern. physiol. et biochim., 64*, 135.
Ledoux, L., J. Le Clerc and J. Brachet, (1955) *Exptl. Cell Research, 9*, 338.
Lee, N. D., J. T. Anderson, R. Miller and R. H. Williams, (1951) *J. Biol. Chem., 192*, 733.
Leslie, I., (1955) in: E. Chargaff and J. N. Davidson, *The Nucleic Acids*. Vol. 2, Academic Press, New York, p. 1.
Lester, R. L., (1953) *J. Am. Chem. Soc., 75*, 5448.
Lipmann, F., (1949) *Federation Proc., 8*, 597.
Littlefield, J. W. and E. B. Keller, (1957) *J. Biol. Chem., 224*, 13.
Littlefield, J. W., E. B. Keller, J. Gross and P. C. Zamecnik, (1955) *J. Biol. Chem., 217*, 111.
Mandel, H. G., R. Markham and R. E. F. Matthews, (1957), *Biochim. Biophys. Acta, 24*, 205.
Mandel, P., M. Jacob and L. Mandel, (1950) *Bull. soc. chim. biol., 32*, 80.
Markham, R., (1953) *Advances in Virus Research, 1*, 315.
Markham, R. and K. M. Smith, (1949) *Parasitology, 39*, 330.
Martin, E. M. and R. K. Morton, (1956) *Biochem. J. ,64*, 687.
Martin, F. and J. Brachet, (1959) *Exptl. Cell Research, 17*, 399.
Matthews, R. E. F., (1954) *J. Gen. Microbiol., 10*, 521.
Matthews, R. E. F., (1956) *Biochim. Biophys. Acta, 19*, 559.
McLean, J. R., G. L. Cohen and M. V. Simpson, (1956) *Federation Proc., 15*, 312.
McLean, J. R., G. L. Cohen, I. K. Brandt and M. V. Simpson, (1958) *J. Biol. Chem., 233*, 657.
Mirsky, A. E., V. G. Allfrey and M. M. Daly, (1954) *J. Histochem. and Cytochem., 2*, 376.
Needham, J. and D. Needham, (1930) *J. Exptl. Biol., 7*, 317.
Neidhardt, F. C. and F. Gros, (1957) *Biochim. Biophys. Acta, 25*, 513.
Niklas, A. and W. Oehlert, (1956) *Beitr. pathol. Anat. u. allg. Pathol., 116*, 92.
Northrop, J. H., (1953) *J. Gen. Physiol., 36*, 581.
Oota, Y. and S. Osawa, (1954) *Biochim. Biophys. Acta, 15*, 162.
Oram, V., (1955) *Acta Anat., 25, suppl. 23*, 7.
Pardee, A. B., (1954) *Proc. Natl. Acad. Sci. U.S., 40*, 263.
Pardee, A. B., (1955) *J. Bacteriol., 69*, 233.
Pardee, A. B. and L. S. Prestidge, (1955) *Federation Proc., 14*, 262.
Pileri, A., L. Ledoux and F. Vanderhaeghe, (1959) *Exptl. Cell Research, 17*, 218.
Potter, J. L. and A. L. Dounce, (1956a) *Federation Proc., 15*, 329.
Potter, J. L. and A. L. Dounce, (1956b) *J. Am. Chem. Soc., 78*, 3078.

PRICE, W. H., (1952) *J. Gen. Physiol.*, *35*, 741.
PRICE, W. H., (1954) *Trans. N.Y. Acad. Sci.*, *16*, 196.
RABINOVITZ, M. AND M. E. OLSON, (1956) *Exptl. Cell Research*, *10*, 747.
RICH, A. AND J. D. WATSON, (1954) *Proc. Natl. Acad. Sci. U.S.*, *40*, 759.
RONDONI, P., (1940) *Enzymologia*, *9*, 380.
SCHRAMM, G. AND W. ZILLIG, (1955) *Z. Naturforsch.*, *10b*, 481.
SCHUMAKER, V. N., (1958) *Exptl. Cell Research*, *15*, 314.
SCHUSTER, H. AND G. SCHRAMM, (1958) *Z. Naturforsch.*, *13b*, 698.
SELS-BRYGIER, J., (1958) *Arch. intern. physiol. et biochim.*, *66*, 128.
SIEKEVITZ, P., (1952) *J. Biol. Chem.*, *195*, 549.
SIEKEVITZ, P. AND G. E. PALADE, (1958) *J. Biophys. Biochem. Cytol.*, *4*, 557.
SKREB-GUILCHER, Y., (1955) *Biochim. Biophys. Acta*, *17*, 599.
SMELLIE, R. M. S., W. M. MCINDOE AND J. N. DAVIDSON, (1953) *Biochim. Biophys. Acta*, *11*, 559.
SPIEGELMAN, S., (1956) in: *Proceedings 3rd Intern. Congress of Biochemistry*, C. LIÉBECQ, ed., Academic Press, New York, p. 185.
SPIEGELMAN, S., H. O. HALVORSON AND R. BEN-ISHAI, (1955) in: W. MCELROY AND B. GLASS, *Amino Acid Metabolism*, Johns Hopkins Press, Baltimore, p. 124.
STENRAM, U., (1954) *Acta Anat.*, *22*, 277.
STEPHENSON, M. L. AND P. C. ZAMECNIK, (1956) *Federation Proc.*, *15*, 362.
STEPHENSON, M. L., K. V. THIMANN AND P. C. ZAMECNIK, (1956) *Arch. Biochem. Biophys.*, *65*, 194.
STICH, H., (1951) *Z. Naturforsch.*, *6 b*, 319.
STRAUB, F. B. AND A. ULLMANN, (1957) *Biochim. Biophys. Acta*, *23*, 665.
STRAUB, F. B., A. ULLMANN AND G. ACS, (1955) *Biochim. Biophys. Acta*, *18*, 439.
SWENSON, P. A., (1950) *Proc. Natl. Acad. Sci. U.S.*, *36*, 699.
SZAFARZ, D., (1952) *Arch. intern. physiol. et biochim.*, *60*, 196.
TAKAHASHI, W. N. AND M. ISHII, (1952) *Phytopathology*, *42*, 690.
TAKAHASHI, W. N. AND M. ISHII, (1953) *Am. J. Botany*, *40*, 85.
TAMM, I., (1958) personal communication.
TITOVA, V. AND V. S. SHAPOT, (1955) *J. Gen. Physiol.*, *39*, 533.
TURIAN, G., (1956) *Experientia*, *12*, 24.
TYNER, E. P., C. HEIDELBERGER AND G. A. LE PAGE, (1952) *Cancer Research*, *12*, 158.
VENDRELY, R., (1946) in: *Un Symposium sur les Protéines*, Masson, Paris, p. 165.
VOLKIN, E., L. ASTRACHAN AND J. L. COUNTRYMAN, (1958) *Virology*, *6*, 545.
WADE, H. E., (1952) *J. Gen. Microbiol.*, *7*, 24.
WEBSTER, G. C., (1955) *Plant Physiol.*, *30*, 351.
WEBSTER, G. C., (1956) *Federation Proc.*, *15*, 380.
WEBSTER, G. C. AND M. P. JOHNSON, (1955) *J. Biol. Chem.*, *217*, 641.
WIAME, J. M., R. STORCK AND E. VANDERWINKEL, (1955) *Biochim. Biophys. Acta*, *18*, 353.
ZAMECNIK, P. C. AND E. B. KELLER, (1954) *J. Biol. Chem.*, *209*, 337.
ZAMECNIK, P. C., E. B. KELLER, J. W. LITTLEFIELD, M. B. HOAGLAND AND R. B. LOFTFIELD, (1956) *J. Cellular Comp. Physiol.*, *47*, suppl. *I*, 81.
ZILLIG, W., W. SCHÄFER AND S. ULLMANN, (1955) *Z. Naturforsch.*, *10b*, 199.

Chapter 2

The Role of Ribonucleic Acids in Growth
and Morphogenesis

After a brief discussion of the possible part played by RNA in
fertilization and cleavage, we shall concentrate on the relationships
between RNA and primary morphogenesis, the accent being placed
on the induction of the nervous system by the organizer in amphibians.

1. FERTILIZATION AND EARLY CLEAVAGE

There is little evidence that RNA plays a direct role in the fertilization of the egg. As we have already seen, ripe spermatozoa probably contain no RNA at all. However, it is possible that, as in the
case of phage infection in bacteria, the egg reacts to the penetration
of the spermatozoön by the production of new RNA or, at any
rate, by a change in RNA metabolism. In fact, Elson et al. (1954)
have observed a decrease in the RNA content following fertilization
of sea urchin eggs. But more sensitive methods involving fertilization of eggs whose RNA has been previously labeled would be
required in order to study changes comparable to those which
occur in bacteria when they are infected by a phage. Such methods
are available but they have not yet been used for this type of study.
In any event, it would be of interest to see how far the analogy
between phage infection and fertilization could be pushed, for in
both cases the essential event is the injection of the genetic material
in the form of DNA into the recipient cell.

Work done by Shaver (1953) on parthenogenesis in amphibian
eggs also suggests that RNA might play a role in fertilization. The
famous experiments of Bataillon (1910) have shown that mere prick-

ing of the unfertilized egg is not sufficient to produce partheno-genetic development. A "second factor" is required. In Bataillon's experiments, the second factor was the introduction of a nucleate cell into the egg. An aster forms after a while around the injected cell, and the presence of this second aster is of course necessary in order to obtain mitotic cleavage. The experiments of Shaver (1953) have shown that the nucleate cell can be replaced by cytoplasmic granules (mitochondria and microsomes) extracted from a variety of cells (testis, red blood cells, frog embryos at stages later than the blastula, etc.). The fact that these granules are inactivated by ribo-nuclease strongly suggests that RNA is somehow involved in the activity of the granules and thus in the formation of the asters.

Experiments with ribonuclease have also been carried out in the case of egg cleavage and have shown that RNA is definitely involved in mitosis and, therefore, in growth processes. It was first found by Thomas *et al.* (1946) that pricking fertilized eggs with a needle which had been dipped in a solution containing ribonuclease stops cleavage. More careful experiments, which involved the micro-injection of known amounts of the enzyme into one of the blasto-meres at the 2–4-cell stage, were performed by Ledoux *et al.* (1955). Finally, it was observed by Brachet and Ledoux (1955) that ribo-nuclease easily penetrates into cleaving eggs as into so many other cells (see Chapter 1). All one has to do is to place a morula in a ribonuclease-containing solution and observe the subsequent cleavages. As shown in Fig. 18 (p. 61), mitosis is completely arrested in the outer blastomeres. The swollen nuclei remain in the inter-phase and it is exceptional for destruction of an already existing mitotic apparatus to be found. It has been observed by Chèvre-mont and Chèvremont-Comhaire (1955) that ribonuclease exerts a similar effect in tissue cultures: cell division quickly stops in fibro-blasts with the nuclei again blocked in interphase. An interesting fact, observed by Chèvremont *et al.* (1956), is that DNA synthesis is not interrupted in these blocked nuclei; their DNA content slowly reaches 4 times the value found for the spermatozoon, but no mitosis follows. It is not known whether the same situation also occurs in amphibian eggs, since measurements of the DNA content of the cell nucleus are difficult during early cleavage. All one can say is that the Feulgen reaction is of apparently normal intensity in the swollen interphase nuclei of the blocked eggs. The facts that, according to Brachet and Ledoux (1955), ribonuclease produces an 85% inhibition of the incorporation of amino acids into proteins in amphibian eggs and that, according to autoradiographic observations, this incorporation is almost entirely limited to the nuclei during early cleavage, shows that the synthesis of the nuclear proteins is very sensitive to ribonuclease in cleaving eggs. It is therefore likely that RNA is involved in the synthesis of these nuclear proteins. But the reason why the ribonuclease-treated eggs never enter into prophase remains obscure. One possibility is that ribonuclease might interfere with the reduplication of the centrosome, which is known to contain RNA. Such a hypothesis would agree with the above-mentioned experiments of Shaver (1953) on the nature of the "second factor" in parthenogenesis. But, for the time being, this is no more than a hypothesis and further work is required in order to test it experimentally.

2. RNA AND THE INDUCTION OF THE NERVOUS SYSTEM

As soon as it was shown by Bautzmann et al. (1932) that organizers killed with alcohol, heating or freezing are still capable of inducing a neural tube, it was realized that induction must be a chemical process and attempts have been made to identify and isolate the "active" inducing substance in pure form. Experiments by Wehmeier (1934) and Holtfreter (1935) gave considerable hope that such a goal might be reached. They found that the "inducing substance" (also called the "evocator") is a very widespread one. Almost all tissues of adult vertebrates and invertebrates, especially if they have been killed beforehand, induce neuralization of the ectoblast if they are grafted into the blastocoele cavity of young gastrulae.

The next step, as was quickly realized by Needham, Waddington, F. G. Fischer, Barth and others, was to try to isolate the inducing substance from an adult tissue, e.g. liver. The results were, however,

References p. 90/93

disappointing, since it soon became clear that many chemically unrelated substances (sterols, glycogen, nucleotides, fatty acids, etc.) can induce neural differentiation in ventral ectoderm (see Brachet, 1944, for a detailed review of this work).

It has been suggested by Brachet (1944) that ribonucleoproteins might play a leading role in neural induction for the following reasons. Ribonucleoproteins extracted from different tissues are better neural inductors than proteins which have a lower RNA content. Tobacco mosaic virus, which is a pure ribonucleoprotein, is a very good inductor (Fig. 19, p. 61). Furthermore, removal of RNA from the active ribonucleoproteins by a ribonuclease digestion leads to a decrease in the inducing activity (Brachet, 1944).

The strong inducing power of ribonucleoproteins (*e.g.* liver microsomes, tobacco mosaic virus) has been confirmed by many workers (Brachet *et al.*, 1952; Kuusi, 1953; Yamada, 1958a, b, etc.). But, on the other hand, it has proved impossible to confirm the inhibitory effect of ribonuclease on abnormal inductors in later experiments (Brachet *et al.*, 1952; Kuusi, 1953; Yamada and Takata, 1955a; Engländer and Johnen, 1957; etc.). The reason for the discrepancy between our first results (1944) and those of more recent workers is now clear; as shown by Hayashi (1958), a short treatment of the ribonucleoprotein with proteolytic enzymes, such as pepsin or trypsin, is enough to destroy the inducing power. At the time of our first experiments (1944), no crystalline ribonuclease was available and there is no doubt that the "purified" preparations used in these experiments were contaminated with proteolytic enzymes. That the active substance in ribonucleoprotein is protein rather than RNA is further shown by the fact that RNA isolated by mild methods (Yamada and Takata, 1955b; Tiedemann and Tiedemann, 1956) from various tissues, including embryos, is a mild inductor only. These negative experiments carry, however, no great weight in view of the difficulty often experienced in isolating non-denaturated RNA.

Although there is, as we have just seen, strong evidence for the view that the active portion in ribonucleoproteins is protein rather than RNA, the question should not yet be considered as completely answered in view of the recent work of Niu (1956, 1958a, b). He demonstrated that explants of the chordomesoblast (organizer) produce ribonucleoproteins in the surrounding medium; the latter —which Niu (1956) calls a "conditioned medium"—induces neuralization in explanted ectoblastic fragments. This neuralization, according to Niu (1956), cannot be explained on the basis of a release of an inducing or toxic substance by cytolyzing cells. Furthermore, ribonuclease inactivates the neuralizing factor produced by the explanted organizer in *Axolotl* and *Triturus torosus*. The enzyme has no inhibitory action, however, in the case of *Triturus rivularis*.

Niu's (1958a, b) most recent papers show how controversial the question of the role of RNA in induction remains. Working with small explanted ectoblastic fragments, he studied the inducing activity of ribonucleoproteins and purified RNA extracted from various sources, especially thymus. He found that these preparations are active and that a treatment with trypsin inactivates them; but the effect of trypsin is apparently not on the nucleoprotein but on the explanted cells themselves, since it can be suppressed by the addition of soya bean trypsin inhibitor. Treatment of the extracts with ribonuclease produces only partial removal (40–70%) of the RNA and reduces the inducing activity. Niu's (1958a, b) conclusion is exactly the opposite of that of Yamada (1958a, b) who believes that there is a correlation between the amount of RNA and the frequency of embryonic differentiation. Obviously, much more work is required before a definite and general conclusion can be reached.

In the foregoing discussion, only facts related to *neural* induction have been presented. The evidence presented suggests that the inductor is a ribonucleoprotein, in which the protein part may be more important than the nucleic acid part. Such a conclusion would not be valid for the induction of *mesodermic* tissues, which is so conspicuous when caudal (and not cephalic) regions are induced. All the available evidence suggests that the caudal organizer is of a purely protein nature (Yamada, 1958a, b).

If we wish to summarize present knowledge concerning the inducing substances, all we can say is that its chemical nature remains obscure and that it will be an exceedingly difficult task to try

References p. 90/93

to elucidate it along the lines that have just been discussed. The menace of an unspecific release of a neuralizing substance which is already present in the ectoblast in a masked form, will always loom before the experimenter. The more complex the experiments become, the more difficult is their interpretation. For instance, inhibition of induction by agents such as ribonuclease, proteolytic enzymes, etc., may be due to an effect on the ectoblast cells themselves, rather than to the block of a specific chemical group in the inducing substance. The reacting system, *i.e.* the ectoblast, may be directly affected by changes in the surrounding medium in two opposite ways: stimulation of neural differentiation (spontaneous neuralization) or loss of competence, which would make the ectoblast incapable of reacting to inducing stimuli.

In view of these uncertainties and the difficulty in solving them, another approach must be used; this is why many investigators have preferred to study RNA distribution and metabolism in intact eggs, either placed in normal or experimentally changed conditions.

3. DISTRIBUTION OF RNA IN NORMAL AMPHIBIAN EGGS

Because of the quality of the available cytochemical methods, precise observations can be made in the case of RNA distribution during amphibian egg development (Brachet, 1942, 1944). As shown in Fig. 20 (p. 62) a polarity gradient is already visible in the advanced oöcytes and in the unfertilized or freshly fertilized eggs. It decreases from the animal to the vegetal pole. At gastrulation (Figs. 21, 22, pp. 62, 63), a secondary RNA gradient decreasing from dorsal to ventral, superimposes itself on the initial animal-vegetal gradient. As a result of RNA synthesis and morphogenetic movements the two gradients interact with each other. The outcome is the appearance, in the late gastrula and the early neurula (Figs. 22, and 23, p. 63), of very well-defined antero-posterior (cephalocaudal) and dorso-ventral gradients. The latter is especially apparent in the chordomesoblast.

When sections of late gastrulae or early neurulae are examined under high power, a high RNA content is found in the space

Text continued on p. 65

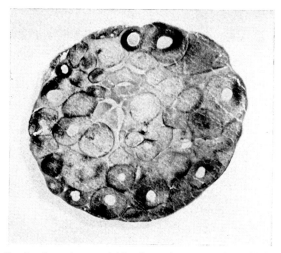

Fig. 18. Swollen interphase nuclei in ribonuclease-treated amphibian morula.
(Brachet and Ledoux, 1955)

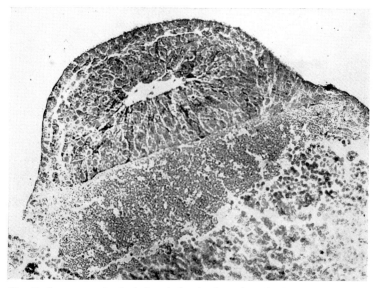

Fig. 19. Large neural tube induced after implantation of tobacco mosaic virus
into the blastocoele cavity of an axolotl gastrula (Brachet, 1950).

References p. 90/93

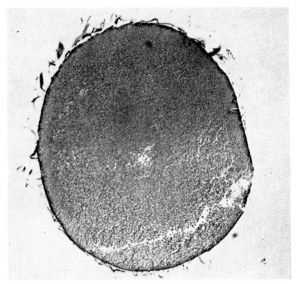

Fig. 20. RNA gradient in fertilized *Xenopus* egg (Brachet, 1957).

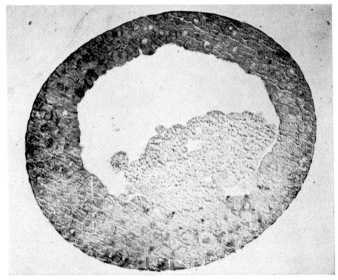

Fig. 21. RNA gradient in *Xenopus* blastula (Brachet, 1957).

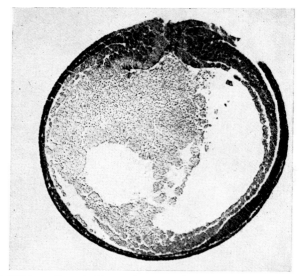

Fig. 22. RNA gradients in *Xenopus* late gastrula. Note the more intensive basophilia of the dorsal lip (right) as compared to the ventral one (Brachet, 1957).

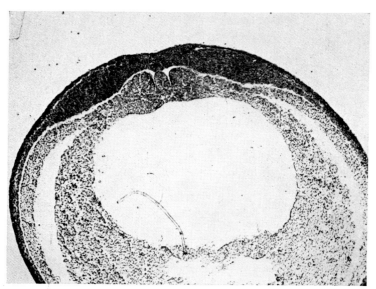

Fig. 23. Dorso-ventral RNA gradients in neurectoderm and chordomesoderm in young neurula of *Xenopus* (Brachet 1957).

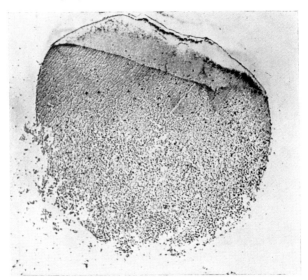

Fig. 24. Disappearance of normal RNA gradient in centrifuged uncleaved egg of *Xenopus;* compare with Fig. 4. The main layers are, from top to bottom: pigment, fats, basophilic hyaloplasm, pigment and yolk.

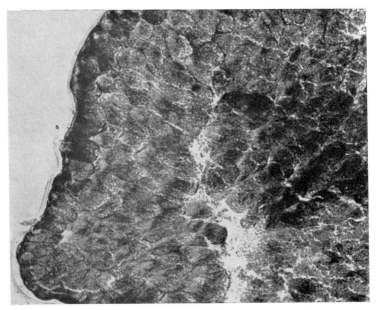

Fig. 25. Local accumulation of RNA in a region which will form a secondary embryo in a centrifuged blastula (Unna staining).

separating the young medullary plate from the presumptive chorda. It looks as if at the exact time of induction, RNA accumulates precisely at the points where the inductor and reacting system are in close contact. Similar observations have also been made more recently in chick embryos (Lavarack, 1957).

At later stages of embryonic development, the RNA content of every organ increases just before its differentiation begins. Differentiation itself (for instance, vacuolization of the notochord or formation of neurones in the nervous system) often results in a drop in the RNA content of the individual cells, except when the latter belong to an actively-synthesizing organ (liver or pancreas, for instance).

Considerable experimental work would be required in order to demonstrate the reality of these gradients—which superimpose themselves on the morphogenetic gradients of the experimental embryologists—quantitatively by means of biochemical methods. The work which has already been done in that direction is sufficient, however, to leave no doubt concerning the existence of the gradients which have been detected by cytochemical methods (Brachet, 1942; Steinert, 1951; Takata, 1953; Flickinger and Blount, 1957). In particular, the work of Flickinger and Blount (1957), who worked with tracer (^{32}P) methods, leads to the important conclusion that new RNA is being synthesized in morphogenetically active regions during differentiation.

It should be pointed out, however, that gradients similar to those which have just been described for RNA have also been detected and described for other substances. Sulfhydryl groups bound to the proteins (Brachet, 1940) and reducing systems (Piepho, 1938; Fischer and Hartwig, 1936; Child, 1948) in particular follow the now familiar dorso-ventral and antero-posterior gradient pattern in their distribution. The same pattern has also been found for oxygen consumption (Sze, 1953), the incorporation of amino acids into proteins (Eakin et al., 1951) and the incorporation of $^{14}CO_2$ into nucleic acids and proteins (Flickinger, 1954). Since mitochondria play a leading part in all processes linked to energy production, it appears likely that these cell organelles are distributed, together

References p. 90/93

with the microsomes, along gradients which superimpose themselves on the morphogenetic gradients. One can, therefore, hardly avoid the conclusion that they represent regions where the yolk reserves are transformed into "true" cytoplasm (ergastoplasm and mitochondria) at a faster rate than elsewhere. From another angle, these gradients should be considered as gradients in the distribution of such cytoplasmic fractions as RNA-rich ergastoplasmic granules or vesicles and mitochondria .

Such a conclusion is reinforced by the recent electron microscope studies of Karasaki (1959), which clearly show that after gastrulation the structure of the mitochondria and the ergastoplasm becomes more and more complicated as differentiation progresses.

Before we can consider these gradients as important factors in morphogenesis, one important question should be answered: are there similar gradients in vertebrate eggs other than those of the amphibians?

The most complete study of RNA distribution in chick embryos is that of Gallera and Oprecht (1948), who showed that node center cells exhibit greater cytoplasmic basophilia than neighbouring cells. These results have been confirmed by Spratt (1952), who used toluidine blue as a stain for RNA detection. We have already seen that in the chick as well as in the amphibian egg, increased basophilia is found at the interface between neuroblast and chordomesoblast, and thus at the very site of induction (Lavarack, 1957).

Gradients in RNA distribution, which are essentially similar to those described for the amphibians, have also been observed in embryos of the fishes (Brachet, 1940, 1942) and the reptiles.

It is beyond the scope of the present book to present the results which have been obtained with mammalian eggs, because the latter are too different from those of the other vertebrates. A few words should, however, be said about the very interesting results obtained by Dalcq and his co-workers on mammalian material. They have been very adequately summarized by Dalcq himself in a recent book (1957).

The cytochemical studies of Dalcq and his school have clearly shown that definite patterns in RNA distribution and synthesis occur during the early development of mammalian eggs, and that, as in other vertebrates, RNA synthesis is especially marked in the mesoblast and the induced parts of the ectoblast.

In short, the cytochemical data obtained in the case of fishes, reptiles, birds and mammals agree very well with the general conclusions which we have drawn from the study of amphibian eggs. RNA is accumulated and is most actively synthesized in the regions of the embryo which have the greatest importance for morphogenetic processes.

We shall now try to answer another important question: what happens to the ribonucleoprotein gradients when morphogenesis or RNA synthesis are experimentally modified?

4. EXPERIMENTAL MODIFICATIONS OF RNA SYNTHESIS AND MORPHOGENESIS: EFFECTS ON RNA GRADIENTS IN AMPHIBIAN EGGS

If synthesis of RNA along animal and vegetal gradients is really an essential factor in morphogenesis, inhibition of RNA synthesis by treatment with *chemical analogues* of purines and pyrimidines should lead to the cessation of development or to abnormal development.

This expectation has been fulfilled, as was first shown by Brachet (1944) in the cases of barbituric acid, benzimidazole and acriflavine. These early studies have been considerably extended by Bieber (1954), Bieber and Hitchings (1955) and Liedke *et al.* (1954, 1957a, b), who used a considerable number (more than one hundred) of chemical analogues of purines, pyrimidines and nucleosides. They usually found inhibition of development at a definite stage. This fact suggests the possibility that new enzymatic mechanisms for RNA synthesis appear at definite stages of development. Of special interest is the fact observed by Liedke *et al.* (1957b) that some of the analogues which were used blocked development at the gastrula stage. If a piece of the arrested gastrula was grafted into a normal gastrula, the blocked fragment resumed normal development and differentiation. We shall find later other examples of such "revitalization" phenomena, when we discuss the develop-

References p. 90/93

ment of eggs which contain an abnormal paternal nucleus (lethal hybrids) or gastrulae which have been submitted to a heat shock. The most likely explanation for this revitalization phenomenon is the same in all these cases. The fragments of the blocked gastrula can no longer synthesize certain substances, RNA in particular, and its development is thus arrested. If it is grafted into a normal gastrula, substances of an unknown nature, but which are required for RNA synthesis, diffuse from the host to the graft.

In chick embryos, inhibitors of RNA synthesis also impair morphogenesis. For instance, Fox and Goodman (1953) found that abnormal synthetic nucleosides, in which ribose was replaced by another sugar (*e.g.* glucose), inhibit the development of explanted chick embryos. Waddington *et al.* (1955) found that the regions which are most sensitive to chemical analogues such as benzimidazole or azaguanine are precisely those which show the highest incorporation of methionine into proteins. Once more, RNA synthesis, protein synthesis and morphogenesis appear as very closely linked in developing eggs.

Finally, Hisaoka and Hopper (1957) have been working on zebra fish eggs and have used barbituric acid as a tool for experimentation. They concluded from these studies that there is a link between morphogenesis and RNA synthesis in fish eggs as well as in those of the amphibians and the chick.

Substances other than purine and pyrimidine analogues have comparable effects. For instance, the well-known inhibitors of oxidative phosphorylation, *dinitrophenol* and *usnic acid*, completely inhibit morphogenesis. The inhibition can be largely reversed if the treated eggs are returned to normal medium. However, abnormalities (persistent yolk plug, microcephaly) can often be found in these cases (Brachet, 1954). Cytochemical (Brachet, 1954) and quantitative (Steinert, 1953) studies have clearly shown that inhibition of development and RNA synthesis always go hand in hand. When the dinitrophenol-treated embryos are returned to normal medium, RNA synthesis is resumed, but only if morphogenesis also takes place.

Another group of interesting substances is that of the steroid hormones (stilboestrol, oestradiol, testosterone), which have been studied by Töndury (1947), Cagianut (1949) and Rickenbacher (1956). These substances inhibit cleavage or make it abnormal. Furthermore, they also modify the normal gradient of RNA distribution. It seems that, owing to alterations of the mitotic apparatus during early cleavage, RNA becomes unevenly distributed in daughter cells. At later stages, strong abnormalities of development can be found, the most conspicuous being unequal differentiation of the medullary folds, which results in an asymmetry of the nervous system. It is a very interesting fact, which certainly deserves much more extensive study, that, according to Cagianut (1949), addition of yeast RNA to embryos which have been treated with steroid hormones definitely improves their differentiation.

Something should be said about another chemical, which is famous among embryologists for the fact that it inhibits the development of chorda and produces strong microcephaly. This is the *lithium* ion, which has been studied in detail from the viewpoint of morphogenesis by Lehmann (1938), Pasteels (1945) and Hall (1942). As a consequence of their work, it is now generally admitted that lithium ions exert their primary effect on the organizer itself, which shows a reduced capacity for induction. The competence of the ectoblast, *i.e.* its capacity to react to the inducing stimuli emanating from a normal organizer, are well known to all embryologists. The most spectacular effects of lithium are the total absence of the chorda (the somites having fused together under the neurula tube) and microcephaly which can be so marked as to lead to cyclopia.

Cytochemical and biochemical studies made on lithium-treated amphibian eggs have yielded a number of important results. First of all, Ficq (1954b) used a very original autoradiography method, based on the nuclear reactions undergone by lithium when it is placed in a neutron flux, to detect lithium in early gastrulae. She found that in lithium-treated gastrulae lithium ions are accumulated by the dorsal half. More recent work by Dent and Sheppard (1957) has largely confirmed Ficq's pioneer experiments of 1954. Strong accumulation of lithium in the medullary plate was also observed by these authors.

References p. 90/93

Biochemical and cytochemical work by Lallier (1954) and by Thomason (1957) has clearly shown that lithium interferes with RNA distribution and synthesis in amphibian eggs. According to Lallier (1954), lithium decreases the RNA gradients, whereas in Thomason's (1957) work, this ion was found to inhibit markedly the incorporation of ^{32}P into the nucleoprotein fraction.

It would, however, be an over-simplification to believe that lithium acts in a *specific* way on nucleic acid distribution and synthesis. For instance, Lallier (1954) has observed that lithium inhibits the dehydrogenases of the tricarboxylic acid cycle, while Ranzi (1957a, b) has produced a considerable amount of evidence for the view that lithium radically modifies the physical properties of the fibrous proteins present in the egg.

We have seen, in the foregoing, that RNA synthesis and distribution on the one hand and morphogenesis on the other appear to be very closely linked processes in developing amphibian and chick eggs treated with a great variety of chemical inhibitors. We shall now consider the effects of *physical* treatments, such as centrifugation, heating or changing the pH of the surrounding medium, on the RNA gradients.

Centrifuging developing eggs is an easy way to modify both the gradient distribution of substances or cell organelles, and morphogenesis. The most important experiments in this field are those of Pasteels (1940, 1953), who worked with amphibian eggs. He found that centrifugation of freshly fertilized eggs leads to the formation of "hypomorph" embryos. They show deficiencies in the nervous system which may go from complete absence to strong microcephaly. When gastrulation of these centrifuged embryos is normal, the result is the production of embryos which have an almost normal tail, but practically no head. On the other hand, centrifugation of blastulae leads to the formation of double or even triple embryos (Pasteels, 1953).

Unpublished studies of Pasteels and Brachet have shown that the centrifugation of both freshly fertilized eggs and blastulae produces profound changes in the distribution of RNA. As shown in Fig. 24 (p. 64), ribonucleoproteins accumulate at the animal pole when fertilized, but still uncleaved, eggs are centrifuged. If these eggs cleave normally, the blastoporal lip forms in a normal position. But the material which invaginates and which corresponds to the organizer is much poorer in RNA than is the organizer in normal eggs. This reduction in the RNA content of the invaginated material is accompanied by a marked decrease in its inducing activity. The hypomorphoses described by Pasteels (1940) are the logical result of such a situation.

Very different results are obtained when blastulae are centrifuged. First there is a collapse of the blastocele roof and an accumulation of RNA-rich material at the centrifugal pole of the cells. Later on, foci of strong RNA synthesis, which are characterized by their very strong basophilia, make their appearance (Fig. 25, p. 64). Finally, an accessory nervous system forms in each of their basophilic areas.

Further investigations, with autoradiography as the major tool, are required in order to analyze further the connections existing between RNA distribution and synthesis on one hand and morphogenesis on the other hand in centrifuged eggs. There is no doubt, however, that the present evidence confirms the view that RNA and morphogenesis are intimately linked processes.

The same conclusion can be drawn from experiments in which a young amphibian gastrula is submitted to a "heat shock" (i.e. heating for one hour at temperatures ranging from 36° to 37° according to the species). We have shown (Brachet, 1948, 1949a, b) that a mild heat shock produces a reversible inhibition of development. When development again proceeds, numerous malformations are found. These abnormalities are essentially similar to those produced by treatment with lithium chloride.

If the temperature chosen is a little higher, the block in development is irreversible, but no cytolysis can be detected for 2–3 days (Fig. 26, p. 73). If a piece of the blocked gastrula is placed in contact with cells of a normal gastrula, even when they belong to another species, a dramatic "revitalization" of the heated cells occurs. As shown in Fig. 27 (p. 74), the organizer of a heated frog gastrula becomes almost normal again. Differentiation into notochord, somites and archenteron roof occurs in the graft, as well as induc-

References p. 90/93

tion of a secondary nervous system. The inductive power of the heated organizer is, however, subnormal, because it has lost the power of inducing a head, but has retained that of spinocaudal induction (Takaya, 1955). "Revitalization" of ectoblast cells from a heated gastrula can also be demonstrated when the cells are placed in contact with a normal organizer. These cells can still react to inducing stimuli by differentiation into a neural plate.

Cytochemical and biochemical studies of gastrulae which have been submitted to an irreversible or a reversible heat shock have disclosed the fact that the RNA gradients are affected to varying degrees according to the severity of the treatment. These gradients become very irregular, while mitotic activity stops and the mitotic apparatus degenerates. When a fragment of the irreversibly heated gastrula is grafted into a normal host, the first sign of healing is an impressive resumption of nucleolar and cytoplasmic basophilia, which precedes the reappearance of mitotic activity. In the reversible heat shocks, the abnormalities found in the distribution of the RNA gradients easily explain why further development becomes abnormal.

Quantitative estimations of the RNA content (Steinert, 1951) have shown that, as suggested by cytochemical observations, RNA synthesis is completely inhibited in the irreversibly blocked gastrulae; if the heat shock is too severe, cytolysis begins after 3 days and the RNA content begins to drop. Steinert's (1951) results have been confirmed by Hasegawa (1955) who demonstrated that in amphibian eggs RNA synthesis is much more sensitive to heating than DNA synthesis. This finding of Hasegawa (1955) is again in excellent agreement with the cytochemical findings.

There is thus no doubt that the ribonucleoprotein structures of the amphibian egg cytoplasm are particularly sensitive to heating. In fact, Brachet (1949a) was able to show that a large proportion of the RNA which is normally found in the microsome fraction appears in the supernatant liquid when heated gastrulae are homogenized and submitted to differential centrifugation. It would, however, be unwise to believe that heat shocks act in a *specific* way on RNA-containing structures. At the gastrula stage, these shocks

Text continued on p. 77

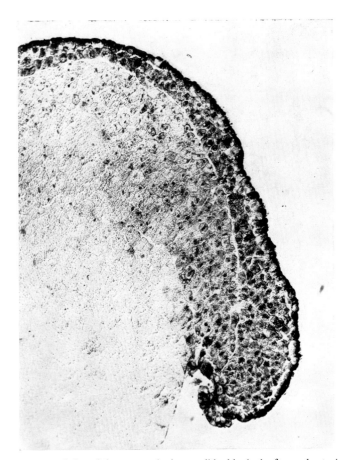

Fig. 26. Dorsal lip of frog gastrula irreversibly blocked after a heat shock (Brachet, 1957).

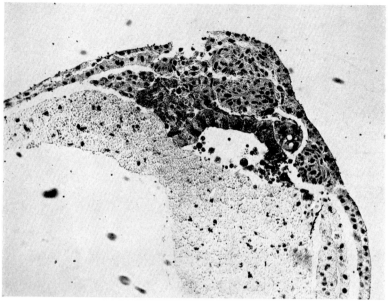

Fig. 27. The organizer of a gastrula blocked by a heat shock has been grafted into a normal host: it has differentiated into chorda and intestinal lumen and it has induced somites and neural masses (Brachet, 1957).

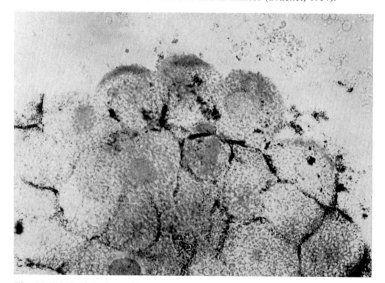

Fig. 28. RNA-rich, basophilic crescents forming in ectoderm cells which have been exposed to an alkaline shock (Brachet, 1957).

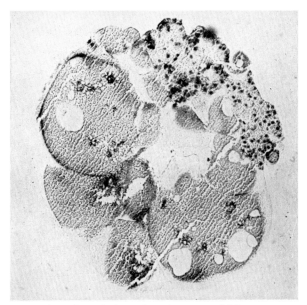

Fig. 29. Formation of atypical ectoderm in an amphibian egg treated with ribonuclease at the morula stage (Brachet and Ledoux, 1955).

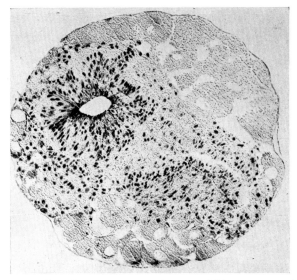

Fig. 30. Formation of a nervous system in an amphibian egg treated with a mixture of RNA and ribonuclease at the morula stage (Brachet and Ledoux, 1955).

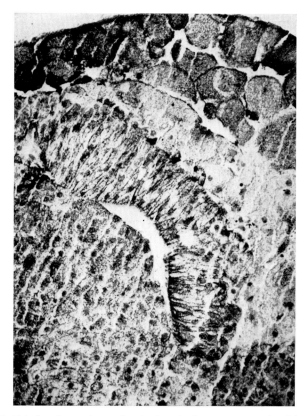

Fig. 31. Ectodermless embryo after treatment of a young gastrula with a mixture of ribonuclease and versene. A chorda has differentiated but the ectoderm cells are blocked and cytolysing (Brachet, 1959).

also produce a very appreciable decrease (30–40%) in the oxygen consumption (Brachet, 1949a).

Once again, it is clear that new tools such as electron microscopy and autoradiography should be used in the case of heated amphibian gastrulae. Electron microscopy could give very valuable information about the alterations which probably occur in the ultra-fine structure of the mitochondria and the basophilic cytoplasmic constituents. Autoradiography, on the other hand, might throw useful light on the more dynamic aspects of nucleic acid and protein synthesis in heated gastrulae. But, whatever the results given by these new methods, the present conclusion will certainly remain valid. Changes in morphogenesis and in RNA distribution and synthesis are always parallel in heated embryos.

It is a well-established fact that *sublethal cytolysis* produced by shifts in the pH or removal of the calcium ions of the medium can provoke the spontaneous neuralization of ectoblastic explants (Holtfreter, 1947). The treatments used by Holtfreter (1947) produce effects which resemble superficially the abnormalities produced by heat shocks, since they are also of short duration and applied at the early gastrula stage. However, heat shocks differ from the acid and alkaline shocks used by Holtfreter (1947) in that they never produce spontaneous neuralization (Mookerjee, 1953). Thus heat shocks decrease the morphogenetic potential of ex-planted ectoblastic fragments, while acid and alkaline shocks often increase it.

Too little is known as yet about the chemical and ultra-structural changes induced by acid and alkaline shocks for any definite conclusions to be drawn. All that can be said is that they modify the structure of the cells in much the same way as does the centrifugation of blastulae. As shown in Fig. 28 (p. 74), the RNA-rich cytoplasm, in the cells which have been exposed to an acid or alkaline medium, accumulates in the form of a basophilic crescent (Brachet, 1946). As we have already seen, the local concentration of RNA at one pole of the cells is a characteristic feature of both normal induction and formation of additional embryonic axes in centrifuged blastulae. It can thus be supposed that the crescent-shaped accumulation of RNA-rich cytoplasm in cells which have been submitted to acid or alkaline shocks has something to do with spontaneous neuralization.

A good correlation between morphogenesis and RNA synthesis is also found when an egg is fertilized by a spermatozoön belonging to another species with the production of a lethal hybrid, or by more than one spermatozoön (polyspermy). RNA synthesis stops when development of the lethal hybrid is blocked, usually as a gastrula. There is a resumption of this synthesis when a fragment of the lethal hybrid becomes "revitalized" after it has been transplanted into a normal host.

Finally, dispermic eggs are often formed of a diploid and a haploid half. If the two halves are equally well developed, their RNA content is the same. But when the haploid half is underdeveloped, its RNA content is lower than that of the diploid half. In the case of dispermic eggs, it is clear that RNA synthesis is not linked to the diploid or haploid condition *per se*, but to the degree of morphogenesis which has been attained by diploid and haploid organs.

In summary, all the evidence that we have concerning RNA distribution and synthesis in normal and experimental embryos (action of numerous chemical substances, centrifugation, heating, treatment with acid or alkali, production of an abnormal nuclear condition, etc.) shows that these phenomena are always closely linked to morphogenesis. One should not forget, however, that RNA is only one of the many constituents of ribonucleoprotein particles. There is no proof, for the time being, that RNA is in itself more important for morphogenesis than the proteins and lipids with which it is associated in ergastoplasmic structures. The advantages of RNA over the other unknown constituents of basophilic structures are the relative ease of its cytochemical detection and its important role in protein synthesis. In any event, experiments designed to demonstrate in an unambiguous way the role of RNA itself in morphogenetic processes are highly desirable.

Brachet and Ledoux (1955) and Brachet (1959) have attempted to attack directly this important problem by treating living amphibian eggs with ribonuclease. It was hoped that the enzyme might penetrate into the living cells, inactivate or break down the RNA which they contained and exert important morphogenetic effects. As we shall see, these hopes have not been entirely fulfilled because of the poor penetration of ribonuclease into amphibian eggs once cleavage is over.

We have already seen that ribonuclease quickly inhibits cleavage in amphibian eggs and that the nuclei are usually blocked in interphase. The penetration of the enzyme is, however, slow and incomplete. Therefore, only the blastomeres which form the outer layers of the morula are irreversibly blocked in their development. If the treated morulae are returned to the normal medium, after a few hours of treatment with ribonuclease, the innermost blastomeres which surround the blastocele resume cleavage. They finally migrate through the dying or dead outer blastomeres and form an atypical undifferentiated ectoderm (Fig. 29, p. 75). If the eggs are treated with a mixture of ribonuclease and RNA, or if they are placed in a RNA-containing medium after the ribonuclease treatment, one can occasionally obtain the formation of a nervous system (Fig. 30, p. 75). It lies on a bed of large, blocked cells. The experiments are, unfortunately, not reproducible enough to allow definite and general conclusions. However, the fact that we have never obtained a nervous system after treatment with ribonuclease alone, but obtained several "neurulae" after a ribonuclease-RNA treatment, provides a definite indication of a role for RNA in normal induction.

Penetration of ribonuclease at later stages of development is usually very poor and thus little or no effect on morphogenesis is observed. One can, however, occasionally find ribonuclease preparations which are more active than others. Since their effects can be duplicated by adding small amounts of versene (EDTA) to otherwise inactive preparations of ribonuclease, it is probable that the active preparations contain some chelating agent as a contaminant.

When blastulae or gastrulae are treated with ribonuclease reinforced by the addition of versene (at low concentrations at which versene itself is inactive), the first visible result is that the ectoderm cells dissociate, lose their basophilia and finally cytolyze (Brachet, 1959). The consequence is the formation of "ectodermless embryos", which have well-differentiated chorda and somites, but no nervous system (Fig. 31, p. 76) or a very reduced one. It was also found in further experiments that cells of the organizer exhibit a marked differential susceptibility towards the ribonuclease-versene mixture. An explanted organizer cytolyzes much more quickly in this medium than explanted ventral mesoblast.

The fact that it is possible, after gastrulae have been treated with ribonuclease and versene, to obtain embryos which have no nervous system should not be taken as a proof that RNA is necessary for inductive processes in the normal organizer. Of course, even a fully active organizer cannot produce its inductive effects unless the ectoderm cells of the reacting system are present. In the experiments just described (Brachet, 1959), the absence of induction is obviously due to the pealing off of the ectoderm cells. Nevertheless, the experiments have some interest in suggesting that the cement or matrix which holds the ectoderm cells together might be of a ribonucleoprotein nature. We shall return to this point a little later in this chapter.

Since it is clear that it is not an easy task to establish, with ribonuclease as a specific agent, whether RNA is directly involved in induction or not, more indirect methods of attack must be employed in the future. Studies of the effects exerted by specific analogues (which inhibit RNA or protein synthesis) on the inducing activity of explanted or implanted organizers might be rewarding for that purpose.

5. PHYSICAL PROPERTIES OF THE INDUCING AGENT: THE POSSIBLE ROLE OF MICROSOMES IN INDUCTION

We owe to Raven (1938) the demonstration of the important fact that the inducing principle can diffuse from cell to cell. If a non-inducing fragment of presumptive ectoderm is left for some hours in contact with the living organizer, it acquires inducing capacities.

These striking experiments of Raven (1938) have led Dalcq (1941) and Needham (1942) to the very interesting hypothesis that the action of the inducing agent might be similar to that of viruses. The well-known fact that the medullary plate which has been induced by the organizer acts as an inductor if it is grafted into the blastocele of a young gastrula leads to the same conclusion. It looks as if the inducing agent can, like a virus, "infect" the neighboring cells, propagate and migrate from one cell to another. A further suggestion has been made by the author (1949): the hypothetical virus might be identical with the microsomes, which have dimensions and a RNA-content comparable to those of many viruses and might therefore possess genetic continuity.

A number of experiments have been performed in recent years in order to test these hypotheses. As we shall now see, they have so far failed to give clearcut answers.

The most direct experiment carried out to test the "microsomes-virus hypothesis" was the isolation of microsomes by ultracentrifugation of homogenates and the microinjection of these particles into a ventral blastomere of a young morula. Such experiments have been attempted by Brachet and Shaver (1949) and by Brachet *et al.* (1952). But the results were rather disappointing, although a local increase of basophilia in the injected blastomeres was often observed. Very few embryos, out of several hundreds, formed a nervous system on the ventral side and it is likely that these few cases resulted from purely mechanical troubles of the gastrulation movements rather than from true induction. It should, however, be added that the experimental conditions adopted for the isolation of the microsome pellet were far from ideal; the temperature in the ultracentrifuge was relatively high and saccharose was not added to the homogenization medium.

Very recently, Yamada (personal communication) has isolated microsomes under much better isolation conditions from amphibian embryos. Adding them to small ectodermic explants, he found that they have a strong inductive (archencephalic) activity.

Some evidence for the view that substances of high molecular weight can diffuse (if only for a short distance) from cell to cell in

References p. 90/93

amphibian gastrulae can be found in our vital staining experiments of 1950. When ectoblast fragments or chordoblast fragments of a young gastrula are placed in neutral red for some time, only the cytoplasmic granules (yolk platelets, pigment, mitochondria and microsomes) are stained. If such a stained fragment is placed in contact by its internal face with an unstained piece, they both stick together and the superficial layer of the unstained fragment quickly becomes coloured. Interposition of a cellophane membrane (which does not prevent diffusion of free neutral red) completely suppresses the diffusion of the dye from the stained fragment to the other one. The embryological interest of these observations is somewhat decreased by the fact that staining is possible in both directions; stained ectoderm as well as stained organizer can be used for such experiments.

These experiments also suffer from the fact that neutral red is of course not a natural constituent of living cells and that its use might lead to a very artificial situation and thus to misleading conclusions. It is for this reason that similar experiments have been performed by Ficq (1954a) with radio-isotopes as markers and an autoradiography technique for detection. By grafting into a normal gastrula an organizer in which either RNA or proteins had previously been labeled, appreciable radioactivity was found in the induced neural tube. The experiments suggest a passage of intact ribonucleoproteins from the organizer into the induced tissue. Unfortunately, the primary neural tube of the host also had measurable radioactivity. This observation indicates that part of the radioactive material is broken down (perhaps as a result of limited cytolysis in the implanted organizer) and re-utilized by the host's neural tube. Similar results have been obtained in Waddington's laboratory by several workers (Waddington and Sirlin, 1955; Sirlin et al., 1956; Pantelouris and Mulherkar, 1957). They conclude that there is no large scale diffusion of macromolecules from the organizer to the induced tissues during induction. Their autoradiography experiments, however, cannot exclude a passage of ribonucleoprotein macromolecules from the inducer to the reacting cells, but this can only occur on a small scale.

This question has been taken up more recently by Rounds and Flickinger (1958) and Flickinger *et al.* (1959), who worked with chemical and immunological methods. Their experiments indicate that in explantations there is a definite (but quantitatively small) transfer of nucleoproteins from mesoderm to ectoderm. Of special interest are experiments in which *Taricha* ectoderm was cultivated in contact with *Rana* mesoderm. Serological tests showed the presence of *Rana* antigens in *Taricha* ectoderm, which again indicates a passage of nucleoproteins from mesoderm to ectoderm. It certainly would be very interesting to follow cytochemically this process with methods involving labeled antibodies.

These autoradiography and serological experiments are in good agreement with our earlier results with vital dyes, since staining was only visible in cells which were adjacent to those of the stained explant. In this case also, there was no large scale transfer of microscopically visible inclusions. The available results thus strongly suggest that exchanges of substances, even of a macromolecular size, occur at the interface separating the inductor from the reacting cells at the late gastrula stage. All these experiments emphasize the importance in induction of either direct contact between cells (Weiss, 1947) or of the intracellular matrix (Grobstein, 1956, 1958). These questions will now be discussed in more detail.

In a very stimulating paper published in 1947, Weiss suggested that an intimate contact between the organizer and the presumptive ectoderm is required for successful induction. The cell membrane would be the main site of the inductive processes. Such a conclusion is, of course, in agreement with all that has just been said about the diffusion of vital dyes and labeled ribonucleoproteins during induction.

There is no doubt that neural induction can be completely suppressed when a cellophane membrane is placed between explants of organizer and ectoblast (Brachet, 1950). Induction stops abruptly when the membrane has interrupted direct contact between the two fragments. Since the membrane used is easily permeable to mononucleotides and slowly permeable to RNA of a molecular weight of about 10,000, it can be concluded that the induction is not due to the diffusion of a substance of low molecular weight. Either direct contact or passage of macromolecules is thus required for successful induction.

Similar results have been obtained and similar conclusions have been drawn by McKeehan (1951) and by De Vicentiis (1952), who worked on the induction of the lens by the eye cup. Again, insertion of a cellophane membrane between inductor and reactor completely stops lens differentiation.

Since membranes with larger pores which would allow free passage of macromolecules also stop lens formation, according to De Vincentiis (1952), it must be admitted that in this case direct contact between inductor and reactor, in the sense which Weiss (1947) suggests, is the essential factor. The situation remains more obscure in the case of primary induction. The large pore membranes used for this purpose by Brachet and Hugon de Scoeux (1949) often produced spontaneous neuralization of the axolotl ectoderm, probably provoking a precytolytic condition. No conclusion can thus be drawn from these experiments, which should be repeated on eggs whose ectoblast is less sensitive to injury than are those of the axolotl.

But, as shown by the work of Grobstein (1955, 1956), direct contact between inducing and reacting cells is not always required for induction. Working on the induction of tubules in metanephrogenic mesenchyme, he found that the inducing stimulus is not stopped by the interposition of a "millipore" membrane. Such a membrane has large pores compared with those of a cellophane membrane but its pores are not large enough to allow the passage of free cells, although they can become filled with long pseudopodia which, apparently, never come in direct contact (Grobstein, 1955, 1956; Grobstein and Dalton, 1957). The active substance, which cannot cross a cellophane membrane, can act at a distance of more than 80 μ (Grobstein, 1958). For all these reasons Grobstein (1955, 1956) believes that induction is not brought about through direct contact or diffusion of a small molecular weight substance, but through the matrix uniting the cells. Such a conclusion is probably also valid for induction of cartilage by spinal cord, which remains possible in the presence of a millipore filter (Lash and Holtzer, 1958). We see no reason why it should not be considered as a very possible explanation in the case of the primary organizer as well.

From the embryological viewpoint, the intercellular matrix of Grobstein (1955, 1956) is a development of Holtfreter's (1943) surface coat. This matrix is a material which is soluble in alkaline media and which presents a marked elasticity. It is present in the cell cortex, in the fertilized egg, and it holds the cells together thus acting as an intercellular cement. The surface coat becomes reinforced in the dorsal lip at the time of gastrulation. It is still further developed in the neural plate at the neurula stage. Dissolution of the surface coat by weak alkalis (*e.g.* potassium cyanide) results in the separation of the cells which form the embryo. This explains why a treatment of gastrulae with relatively concentrated cyanide solutions produces a dissociation of the cells first at the animal pole, and then in the dorsal lip. The dissociated cells soon undergo cytolysis.

Very little is known, unfortunately, about the chemical nature of the surface coat or the intercellular matrix. Treatment with the calcium-complexing agent versene (EDTA) produces separation of the gastrula cells. This effect of versene, as we have seen earlier, is greatly enhanced by the addition of small amounts of ribonuclease (Brachet, 1959). It is also known that proteolytic enzymes, *e.g.* trypsin, readily dissociate the cells of the amphibian gastrula. After dissociation by various means, a ribonucleoprotein is liberated (Curtis, 1958). This fact suggests that the intercellular matrix is of a ribonucleoprotein nature, although cytolysis of part of the cells would easily explain the results obtained on dissociated cells by Curtis (1958). Cytochemical studies are, however, in favour of Curtis' conclusion that the intercellular cement is a ribonucleoprotein. In amphibian eggs and embryos, cell membranes give very strong reactions for RNA. Pending further experimental and more precise work, it seems safe to conclude that the intercellular matrix is made of a ribonucleoprotein associated with calcium ions and, possibly, mucopolysaccharides. If RNA is really involved in the intercellular matrix composition, its role in induction would become more probable and easier to understand.

References p. 90/93

There is, however, a certain amount of evidence for the view that the induction of neural structure can be obtained also in ectoblast cells treated with *soluble* agents, without direct contact as in the living organizer or killed tissues. We refer now to the above-mentioned experiments of Niu and Twitty (1953) and Niu (1956), who found that if chordomesoblastic and ectoblastic fragments are cultivated side by side but without direct contact of the explants, neuralization of the organizer fragments liberates a diffusible substance which has the spectroscopic properties of a nucleoprotein. As we have already mentioned, the "conditioned medium" in which this nucleoprotein has accumulated is itself neuralizing. In the absence of any chordomesoblastic cell, it produces neural differentiation in ectoblastic explants.

We have seen that in more recent experiments of Niu (1958a, b) the mere addition of ribonucleoprotein or even of RNA from thymus can produce the neuralization of ectoderm explants. It is interesting to note that in the case of RNA the inducing activity is markedly increased when a protein, which is inactive by itself, is mixed with the nucleic acid. This fact strongly suggests that the uptake and subsequent neuralization of the explants is linked to a pinocytosis mechanism which is induced by the protein. We have observed that in organisms which are capable of pinocytosis (*e.g.* amoebae), the uptake of RNA is greatly increased if a protein is added to the medium in order to induce pinocytosis. A careful study of pinocytosis in ectoderm explants placed in various experimental conditions might be rewarding and might throw some light on the mechanisms of induction.

Interesting as they are, these experiments do not carry entire conviction because of the risk of sublethal cytolysis which is always present. Niu and Twitty (1953) and their followers were of course aware of this danger and they thought that they could avoid it. But the fragility of gastrula cells is such that it is extremely difficult to avoid death or injury of a few of the explanted cells even when one works very carefully. Furthermore, results obtained with artificial systems such as those used by Niu and Twitty (1953) and Niu (1956, 1958a, b) can give little information about the processes which occur in a normal embryo. It is important to remember, in this respect, that Holtfreter (1955) found that killed tissues liberate substances which can diffuse through a cellophane membrane and induce the neuralization of ectoblast fragments in contact with the membrane. The killed tissues of Holtfreter (1955) obviously behave quite differently from the living organizer, whose inductive power is stopped by the insertion of a cellophane membrane (Brachet, 1950).

6. THE ROLE OF THE CELL NUCLEUS IN MORPHOGENESIS

There is no doubt that in all vertebrates a very important factor in morphogenesis is the existence of a precise gradient pattern, which involves both RNA (ergastoplasm) and mitochondria. Since RNA and the ATP produced by the mitochondria are two major factors in protein synthesis, it is clear that the above-mentioned animal-vegetal and dorso-ventral gradients must also be gradients of protein synthesis. Autoradiography, especially in the work of Tencer (1958), confirms this expectation. However, dynamic studies on the incorporation of various precursors into nucleic acids and proteins do not give exactly the same picture as the more static methods used for the cytochemical detection of RNA. As already mentioned, they show that incorporation of these precursors is very much greater in the nuclei than in the cytoplasm during cleavage. It appears as if the main job for the egg is to undergo mitoses as fast as possible during this initial phase of development. The result is that synthetic processes are almost reduced to the reduplication of the constituents of chromatin itself. Later on, at gastrulation, synthesis of RNA and proteins becomes evident in the cytoplasm as well as in the nuclei. This synthesis follows the very distinct dorso-ventral and antero-posterior RNA gradients found in the gastrula and the neurula (Tencer, 1958).

It was suggested by the author, as early as 1949, that the changes in metabolism which occur at gastrulation are linked to a new type of interaction between the nucleus and the cytoplasm. During cleavage, biochemical interactions between nuclei and cytoplasm

References p. 90/93

would be kept to a minimum and the dividing nucleus might thus be considered as inactive in so far as the control of anabolic activities is concerned. In other words, during cleavage, the egg would not be very different from an enucleate egg. In fact, it is well known that sea urchin and amphibian eggs can cleave repeatedly in the complete absence of the nucleus (see Brachet, 1957, 1960 for a much more complete discussion of this problem).

At gastrulation, mitotic activity slows down considerably and the nuclei now "have time" to build up nucleoli during interphase. Obviously, synthesis of RNA, as well as that of DNA, must occur in the nuclei from that stage on. Very recent observations from our co-workers Bieliavsky and Tencer (1959) substantiate this expectation. Working with dissociated cells from amphibian blastulae, gastrulae and neurulae, and using incorporation of tritium-labeled uridine and autoradiography as the main tools, they found that this RNA precursor is exclusively incorporated into DNA during cleavage. The eggs are thus capable of utilizing this ribose derivative for DNA synthesis. At gastrulation and afterwards, the labeled uridine is incorporated in both DNA and RNA. In the case of the latter, labeling is stronger in the nuclei than in the cytoplasm.

The view that intricate interactions between the nucleus and the cytoplasm are required in order to obtain morphogenesis at stages following cleavage, is also supported by the fact that in amphibians many hybrid combinations become lethal at the gastrula stage. Despite the presence of an abnormal sperm nucleus, cleavage is perfectly normal. But development stops at the young gastrula stage unless a fragment of the lethal embryo is grafted into a normal gastrula. As pointed out before, such a graft is followed by a "revitalization" of the fragment, in which morphogenesis and RNA synthesis are, as usual, closely linked together. Obviously, the presence of the abnormal nucleus does not permit the synthesis of certain substances which are required for morphogenesis. These substances, which are not species-specific, are supplied by the normal host in the case of a graft, if followed by revitalization. Nothing is known about the nature of these substances, but it might be significant that in the lethal hybrids of both Anurans (Brachet,

1954) and Urodeles (Zeller, 1956), cytochemical methods demonstrate the presence of an excess of RNA in the nuclei of the blocked hybrids. It looks as if an abnormal RNA, which cannot be utilized by the cytoplasm, is synthesized by the foreign nucleus. More will be said about the relationships of nuclear and cytoplasmic RNA in the next chapter.

Before we leave the problem of morphogenesis, a final problem should be briefly discussed (see Brachet, 1957, 1960, for more detailed discussions). Do the nuclei undergo some sort of differentiation during development? Such a differentiation has been postulated by Morgan (1934), who advanced the view that during cleavage equipotential nuclei (thus undifferentiated nuclei) would be distributed in a chemically heterogeneous cytoplasm. Owing to this heterogeneity of the surrounding cytoplasm, genes would be activated in certain nuclei and inactivated in others. The nuclei would then no longer be equipotential but differentiated. Differences in genetic activity among the nuclei would, in turn, produce deeper modifications in the chemical composition of the surrounding cytoplasm, and would ultimately lead to embryonic differentiation.

This theory is well supported by the most remarkable experiments of "nuclear transfer" performed by Briggs and King (1953, 1955, 1957). They were able to inject into an enucleate recipient of unfertilized eggs, the nucleus from a cell taken at the blastula, gastrula or neurula stage. Their main result is that nuclei are equipotential before gastrulation and that they are still undifferentiated at this stage, since they can support normal and complete development. But the nuclei become different from each other and become irreversibly differentiated when a late gastrula stage is reached. Autoradiographic observations on $^{14}CO_2$ incorporation by Tencer (1958) show that nuclear differentiation is closely linked to changes in metabolic activity. In the blastula, despite the existence of the animal-vegetal gradient, all the nuclei become labeled to the same extent. In the gastrula, on the other hand, the intensity of the labeling in the various nuclei becomes parallel to the intensity of the cytoplasmic RNA gradients.

There is thus no doubt that, in the gastrula, strong interactions between the nuclei and the cytoplasm occur and that these inter-actions are linked to the existence of the cytoplasmic RNA gra-dients. The latter thus appear, once more, as extremely important factors in morphogenesis.

REFERENCES

BATAILLON, E., (1910) Compt. rend., 150, 996.
BAUTZMANN, H., J. HOLTFRETER, H. SPEMANN AND O. MANGOLD, (1932) Naturwissenschaften, 20, 971.
BIEBER, S., (1954) J. Cellular Comp. Physiol., 44, 11.
BIEBER, S. AND G. H. HITCHINGS, (1955) Cancer Research, suppl. 3, 80.
BIELIAVSKY, N. AND R. TENCER, (1959) Exptl. Cell Research, (in the press).
BRACHET, J., (1940) Arch. biol. (Liège), 51, 167.
BRACHET, J., (1942) Arch. biol. (Liège), 53, 207.
BRACHET, J., (1944) Embryologie chimique, Desoer, Liège.
BRACHET, J., (1946) Compt. rend. soc. biol., 140, 1123.
BRACHET, J., (1948) Experientia, 4, 353.
BRACHET, J., (1949a) Bull. soc. chim. biol., 31, 724.
BRACHET, J., (1949b) Pubbl. staz. zool. Napoli, 21, 71.
BRACHET, J., (1950) Experientia, 6, 56.
BRACHET, J., (1954) Arch. biol. (Liège), 65, 1.
BRACHET, J., (1957) Biochemical Cytology, Academic Press, New York.
BRACHET, J., (1959) Acta Embryol. Morphol. Exptl., 2, 107.
BRACHET, J., (1960) The Biochemistry of Development, Pergamon Press, London.
BRACHET, J. AND F. HUGON DE SCOEUX, (1949) Journ. cyto-embryol. belgonéerl., Gand, 56.
BRACHET, J. AND L. LEDOUX, (1955) Exptl. Cell Research, suppl. 3, 27.
BRACHET, J. AND J. SHAVER, (1949) Experientia, 5, 204.
BRACHET, J., S. GOTHIÉ AND T. KUUSI, (1952) Arch. biol. (Liège), 63, 429.
BRIGGS, R. AND T. J. KING, (1953) J. Exptl. Zool., 122, 485.
BRIGGS, R. AND T. J. KING, (1955) in: E. BUTLER (ed.), Biological Specificity and Growth, Princeton Univ. Press, p. 207.
BRIGGS, R. AND T. J. KING, (1957) J. Morphol., 100, 269.
CAGIANUT, B., (1949) Z. Zellforsch. u. mikroskop. Anat., 34, 471.
CHÈVREMONT, M. AND S. CHÈVREMONT-COMHAIRE, (1955) Nature, 176, 1075.
CHÈVREMONT, M., S. CHÈVREMONT-COMHAIRE AND H. FIRKET, (1956) Arch. biol. (Liège), 67, 635.
CHILD, C. M., (1948) J. Exptl. Zool., 109, 79.
CURTIS, A. S. G., (1958) Nature, 181, 185.
DALCQ, A., (1941) L'œuf et son dynamisme organisateur, Masson, Paris.
DALCQ, A., (1957) Introduction to General Embryology, Oxford Univ. Press.
DENT, J. N. AND C. W. SHEPPARD, (1957) J. Exptl. Zool., 135, 587.
DE VINCENTIIS, M., (1952) Atti soc. oftalmol. lombarda, 13, 3.
EAKIN, R. M., P. B. KUTSKY AND W. E. BERG, (1951) Proc. Soc. Exptl. Biol. Med., 78, 502.
ELSON, D., T. GUSTAFSON AND E. CHARGAFF, (1954) J. Biol. Chem., 209, 285.
ENGLÄNDER, J. AND A. G. JOHNEN, (1957) J. Embryol. Exptl. Morphol., 5, 1.

FICQ, A., (1954a) *J. Embryol. Exptl. Morphol.*, *2*, 194.
FICQ, A., (1954b) *J. Embryol. Exptl. Morphol.*, *2*, 204.
FISCHER, F. G. AND H. HARTWIG, (1936) *Z. vergleich. Physiol.*, *24*, 1.
FLICKINGER, R. A., (1954) *Exptl. Cell Research*, *6*, 172.
FLICKINGER, R. A., AND R. W. BLOUNT, (1957) *J. Cellular Comp. Physiol.*, *50*, 403.
FLICKINGER, R. A., E. HATTON AND D. E. ROUNDS, (1959) *Exptl. Cell Research*, *17*, 30.
FOX, J. J. AND I. GOODMAN, (1953) *Biochim. Biophys. Acta*, *10*, 77.
GALLERA, J. AND O. OPRECHT, (1948) *Rev. suisse zool.*, *55*, 243.
GROBSTEIN, C., (1955) in: D. RUDNICK, (ed.) *Aspects of Synthesis and Order in Growth*, Princeton Univ. Press, p. 233.
GROBSTEIN, C., (1956) *Exptl. Cell Research*, *10*, 424.
GROBSTEIN, C., (1958) *Exptl. Cell Research*, *13*, 575.
GROBSTEIN, C. AND A. J. DALTON, (1957) *J. Exptl. Zool.*, *135*, 57.
HALL, T. S., (1942) *J. Exptl. Zool.*, *89*, 1.
HASEGAWA, H., (1955) *Nature*, *175*, 1031.
HAYASHI, Y., (1958) *Embryologia*, *4*, 33.
HISAOKA, K. K. AND A. F. HOPPER, (1957) *Anat. Record*, *129*, 297.
HOLTFRETER, J., (1935) *Arch. Entwicklungsmech. Organ.*, *133*, 367.
HOLTFRETER, J., (1943) *J. Exptl. Zool.*, *93*, 251.
HOLTFRETER, J., (1947) *J. Exptl. Zool.*, *106*, 197.
HOLTFRETER, J., (1955) *Exptl. Cell Research*, suppl. *3*, 188.
KARASAKI, S., (1959) *Embryologia*, *4*, 247.
KUUSI, T., (1953) *Arch. biol. (Liège)*, *64*, 189.
LALLIER, R., (1954) *J. Embryol. Exptl. Morphol.*, *2*, 323.
LASH, J. W. AND H. HOLTZER, (1958) *Biol. Bull.*, *115*, 322.
LAVARACK, J. O., (1957) *J. Embryol. Exptl. Morphol.*, *5*, 111.
LEDOUX, L., J. LE CLERC AND J. BRACHET, (1955) *Exptl. Cell Research*, *9*, 338.
LEHMANN, F. E., (1938) *Arch. Entwicklungsmech. Organ.*, *138*, 106.
LIEDKE, K. B., M. ENGELMAN AND S. GRAFF, (1954) *J. Exptl. Zool.*, *127*, 201.
LIEDKE, K. B., M. ENGELMAN AND S. GRAFF. (1957a) *J. Embryol. Exptl. Morphol.*, *5*, 368.
LIEDKE, K. B., M. ENGELMAN AND S. GRAFF, (1957b) *J. Exptl. Zool.*, *136*, 117.
MCKEEHAN, M. S., (1951) *J. Exptl. Zool.*, *117*, 31.
MOOKERJEE, S., (1953) *Experientia*, *9*, 340.
MORGAN, T. H., (1934) *Embryology and Genetics*, Columbia Univ. Press.
NEEDHAM, J., (1942) *Biochemistry and Morphogenesis*, Cambridge Univ. Press.
NIU, M. C., (1956) in: D. RUDNICK, (ed.), *Cellular Mechanisms of Differentiation and Growth*, Princeton Univ. Press, p. 155.
NIU, M. C., (1958a) *Proc. Natl. Acad. Sci. U.S.*, *44*, 1264.
NIU, M. C., (1958b) in: *The Chemical Basis of Development*, Johns Hopkins Press, Baltimore. pp. 256, 625.
NIU, M. C. AND V. C. TWITTY, (1953) *Proc. Natl. Acad. Sci. U.S.*, *39*, 985.
PANTELOURIS, E. M. AND L. MULHERKAR, (1957) *J. Embryol. Exptl. Morphol.*, *5*, 51.
PASTEELS, J., (1940) *Arch. biol. (Liège)*, *51*, 335.

PASTEELS, J., (1945) *Arch. biol. (Liège)*, *56*, 105.
PASTEELS, J., (1953) *J. Embryol. Exptl. Morphol.*, *1*, 5, 125.
PIEPHO, H., (1938) *Biol. Zentr.*, *58*, 90.
RANZI, S., (1957a) in: *The Beginnings of Embryonic Development*, *Publ. Am. Assoc. Advance. Sci.*, Washington, p. 291.
RANZI, S., (1957b) *Année biol.*, *33*, 522.
RAVEN, C. P., (1938) *Arch. Entwicklungsmech. Organ.*, *137*, 661.
RICKENBACHER, J., (1956) *Z. Zellforsch. u. mikroskop. Anat.*, *45*, 339.
ROUNDS, D. E. AND R. A. FLICKINGER, (1958) *J. Exptl. Zool.*, *137*, 479.
SHAVER, J. R., (1953) *J. Exptl. Zool.*, *122*, 169.
SIRLIN, J. L., S. K. BRAHMA AND C. H. WADDINGTON, (1956) *J. Embryol. Exptl. Morphol.*, *4*, 248.
SPRATT, N. T., (1952) *Ann. N.Y. Acad. Sci.*, *55*, 40.
STEINERT, M., (1951) *Bull. soc. chim. biol.*, *33*, 549.
STEINERT, M., (1953) *Thesis*, Univ. of Brussels.
SZE, L. C., (1953) *Physiol. Zoöl.*, *26*, 212.
TAKATA, K., (1953) *Biol. Bull.*, *105*, 348.
TAKAYA, H., (1955) *Proc. Japan Acad.*, *31*, 66.
TENCER, R., (1958) *J. Embryol. Exptl. Morphol.*, *6*, 117.
THOMAS, A. J., J. ROSTAND AND J. GRÉGOIRE, (1946) *Compt. rend.*, *222*, 1139.
THOMASON, D., (1957) *Nature*, *179*, 823.
TIEDEMANN, H. AND H. TIEDEMANN, (1956) *Z. physiol. Chem. Hoppe-Seyler's*, *306*, 132.
TÖNDURY, G., (1947) *Acta Anat.*, *4*, 269.
WADDINGTON, C. H. AND J. L. SIRLIN, (1955) *Proc. Roy. Soc. Edinburgh*, *24*, 28.
WADDINGTON, C. H., M. FELDMAN AND M. M. PERRY, (1955) *Exptl. Cell Research*, *suppl. 3*, 366.
WEHMEIER, E., (1934) *Arch. Entwicklungsmech. Organ.*, *132*, 384.
WEISS, P., (1947) *Yale J. Biol. and Med.*, *19*, 235.
YAMADA, T., (1958a) *Experientia*, *14*, 81.
YAMADA, T., (1958b) in: *The Chemical Basis of Development*, Johns Hopkins Press, Baltimore, p. 217.
YAMADA, T. AND S. TAKATA, (1955a) *Exptl. Cell Research*, *suppl. 3*, 402.
YAMADA, T. AND S. TAKATA, (1955b) *J. Exptl. Zool.*, *128*, 291.
ZELLER, C., (1956) *Arch. Entwicklungsmech. Organ.*, *148*, 311.

Chapter 3

The Role of the Cell Nucleus in RNA and Protein Synthesis

1. HYPOTHESES ON THE BIOCHEMICAL ROLE OF THE NUCLEUS

Many hypotheses concerning the biochemical role of the cell nucleus have been disproved experimentally. For instance, it is no longer held that the nucleus is the main center of cellular oxidations, as Loeb believed in 1899, or that it is a "storehouse" of enzymes, as Wilson concluded in 1925. Removal of the nucleus, in many cases, has no appreciable effect on the oxygen uptake and few enzymes are more concentrated in the nucleus than in the cytoplasm (see Brachet, 1957, for a full discussion of these problems).

More satisfactory is the view already held in 1892 by Verworn that the nucleus is the center of the synthetic activities of the cell, *i.e.* of its anabolism. Verworn's (1892) idea has been made more precise by Caspersson (1941, 1950), who considers the nucleus as a cell organelle especially organized as the *main center for the formation of proteins.* Caspersson's (1941, 1950) theory is based especially on his own cytochemical observations, which established that the nucleolus is well developed and rich in RNA in all cells which are the sites of intensive protein synthesis. This finding has since been abundantly confirmed. According to Caspersson (1941, 1950), cytoplasmic RNA accumulates around the nuclear membrane; that such a perinuclear accumulation of RNA is a universal phenomenon appears somewhat doubtful now.

More recently, Mazia (1952) proposed the new hypothesis that the nucleus is concerned with the *replacement* of the activities of the cell. Mazia's (1952) hypothesis is based on the essentially correct observation that removal of the nucleus is not followed by *imme-*

diate effects on cellular activities, although the latter decrease sooner or later. For Mazia (1952), two alternatives are possible. In the first, the nucleus is the site of enzyme synthesis, as in Wilson's (1925) hypothesis. Removal of the nucleus should then lead to a continuous drop in the enzyme content of the cytoplasm. Such a drop would not necessarily occur at the same rate for all cytoplasmic enzymes, since the latter might be synthesized in different parts of the nucleus. It is also possible, according to Mazia, that enzymes which are functionally related decline together if their replacement mechanisms in the nucleus are somehow related. Still another possibility is that the replacement of coenzymes is a function of the nucleus.

In the second of Mazia's (1952) alternatives, the product of nuclear activity might be a cytoplasmic unit. The latter, which would be comparable to a plasmagene, would play a role in cytoplasmic synthesis; but it would require continuous replacement by the nucleus for its maintenance in the cytoplasm. A similar idea had been expressed before by Wright (1945) and by Marshak (1948); one of its consequences is that the losses of activity after removal of the nucleus would be discontinuous instead of gradual. The discontinuities would occur at the time when the synthetic units were exhausted.

2. AVAILABLE MATERIALS AND METHODS

The ideal method is, of course, to work with living intact cells. This has become feasible now that good autoradiography techniques have become available. It is possible to introduce into the cell a specific precursor of nucleic acids or proteins and to follow its incorporation in the nucleus and the cytoplasm. As we shall see, this method has already yielded a number of important results. But the drawbacks of autoradiography, especially for quantitative work, should be kept in mind. It is seldom possible to measure the specific radioactivity by this method, because it is often unknown how much of the free precursor is present in the part of the cell which is being studied; furthermore, the exact composition of the nucleic acids or proteins present in this part of the cell is usually unknown. To take a specific example, let us suppose that autoradiography shows no incorporation of phenylalanine into the nucleolus. This might mean that the nucleolus is inactive in protein synthesis, but it might equally be due to the fact that free phenylalanine cannot penetrate into the nucleolus (lack of permeability to this amino acid) or to the absence of phenylalanine in the proteins of the nucleolus.

A second way of studying the biochemical role of the cell nucleus is "merotomy": a unicellular organism of sufficient size is cut into two halves and the metabolic activities of the nucleate and enucleate halves are compared. Merotomy is easy to perform on amoebae, on the large alga *Acetabularia*, and on sea urchin or amphibian eggs. Most of the results which are presented later in this chapter were obtained by this method. One should also mention the interesting case of the reticulocytes, for which the enucleation is performed by nature itself during maturation of the red blood cells.

Finally, it is of course possible to work on homogenates. The advantage is that large amounts of nuclei can be obtained, so that micromethods are not a prerequisite, as is the case for the unicellular organisms. But the homogenate method suffers from several draw-backs, such as possible loss or adsorption of enzymes (*e.g.* phosphatase) during isolation. In the absence of adequate electron microscopic observations, it is difficult to be sure that the isolated fractions are really identical with the preexisting intracellular granules; rupture of nuclei or mitochondria, as well as aggregation of smaller cytoplasmic particles, are difficult to avoid completely. Even after very careful work, it is therefore impossible to be certain that the fractions obtained are cytologically homogeneous.

The great limitations of the homogenate method become apparent when, as in this chapter, the interest shifts from a mere description of the chemical composition of the several types of cell organelles to the more dynamic approach exemplified by the question: what is the nature of the *interactions* which occur between the various constituents of the cell, and between the nucleus and the cyto-plasmic particles in particular? It is perfectly legitimate for a bio-chemist to mix together the various fractions obtained by differential centrifugation of homogenates. A system consisting of microsomes and mitochondria has been very useful to Siekevitz (1952) in his studies on the *in vitro* incorporation of amino acids into proteins. Vishniac and Ochoa (1952) have studied, with advantage, the biochemical events which occur when chloroplasts are mixed with mitochondria isolated from animal tissues. Potter *et al.* (1951) and Johnson and Ackermann (1953), in an effort toward an understanding of the biochemical role of the nucleus, have followed the effects of the addition of nuclei on oxidative phosphorylations in mitochondria. They found that, although the nuclei themselves lack respiratory enzymes, they stimulate phosphorylation reactions. Experiments of that type have definite biochemical interest and value but are useless when the nature of the interaction between nuclei, mitochondria and ergastoplasm in the *intact living* cell is our objective. For instance, stimulation of mitochondrial oxidative phosphorylations by the addition of nuclei may simply be caused by an autolytic release of enzymes or cofactors from the nuclei; such a phenomenon might never occur in the nucleus of a living cell. In fact, the indications given by this type of homogenate experiment may be totally misleading if the importance of structural integrity inside the cell is neglected.

In the case of the nuclei at least, there is another reason for doubting the value of the experiments performed on mixed fractions recovered by differential centrifugation of homogenates. If we take as a test of survival for isolated nuclei the capacity of dividing when they are reintroduced into cytoplasm, there is no doubt that isolated nuclei are very quickly inactivated by contact with the outside medium. In experiments by Comandon and De Fonbrune (1939) on the transplantation of a nucleus to an enucleate *Amoeba* fragment, very close contact between the cell surfaces of the donor and the receptor amoebae is indispensable; the slightest contact of the nucleus with the outside medium results in "death" and elimination of the transplanted nucleus. The same is true for the embryonic nuclei transplanted by Briggs and King (1953) into enucleate unfertilized frog eggs; the nucleus must be protected against the medium by the crushed cytoplasm of the cell out of which it is taken if the nuclear transplantation is to be successful. None of the many media tried by Briggs and King (1953) has proved satisfactory so far. Until a medium is found where nuclei can be kept for a long time without losing their biological activities, experiments made on nuclei isolated from homogenates will have limited biological interest only. Such a medium will probably be difficult to find, since we know from the work of Cutter *et al.* (1955) that the nuclei which swim freely in coconut liquid endosperm are only capable of degenerative amitosis.

3. EXPERIMENTAL RESULTS

a. Intact cells

As already mentioned, autoradiography, despite its shortcomings, is the only method which can give information on what happens *in situ* at the cytological level.

All the autoradiographic experiments published so far clearly establish the greater metabolic lability of nuclear RNA compared to that of cytoplasmic RNA. The autoradiographic observations of Ficq (1955a, b) on starfish and frog oöcytes have introduced an important point; the rapid incorporation of labelled adenine or orotic acid into RNA is especially characteristic of the *nucleolus*. In the germinal vesicle of amphibian oöcytes, however, the incorporation of radioactive adenine also proceeds very quickly in the RNA-containing loops of the lampbrush chromosomes (Brachet and Ficq, 1956). In *Acetabularia* also, autoradiographic observations indicate a very rapid incorporation of adenine into the nucleoli (Fig. 32, p. 109).

Similar observations have been made with radioactive phosphate as a label, by Vincent (1954) for starfish oöcytes, by Odeblad and Magnusson (1954) for mouse oöcytes, by Stich and Hämmerling (1953) for *Acetabularia*, and by Taylor (1953, 1954) and Taylor and McMaster (1955) for insect glands.

There is thus no doubt that the nucleus—and especially the nucleolus—is the site of a particularly active RNA anabolism. All these observations are obviously compatible with the view that nucleolar RNA is a precursor of cytoplasmic RNA, but they did not prove the point directly.

However, recent observations of Woods and Taylor (1959), who used tritium-labeled uridine as a specific precursor, are entirely compatible with the view that RNA is synthesized primarily in the nucleus and that cytoplasmic RNA is largely, if not entirely, of nuclear origin; they observed that in plant cells the nuclei are the first to become radioactive. If, at that time, the cells are transferred to a non-radioactive medium, the labeled nuclear RNA can be seen to move progressively toward the cytoplasm. Similar observations have been made by Zalokar (1959) in the case of centrifuged *Neurospora* cells.

Let us now consider protein metabolism. In starfish and amphibian oöcytes, nucleoli incorporate precursors (glycine or phenylalanine) at a faster rate than does either nuclear sap or cytoplasm, according to Ficq (1955a, b). But the differences are never as marked as in the case of the incorporation of purines or pyrimidines into RNA. The same remark can be made for centrifuged amphibian oöcytes. While the incorporation of adenine is, as we have just seen, very intense in the loops of the lampbrush chromosomes, the differences between the loops, the rest of the nuclear sap and the cytoplasm is much less conspicuous for proteins. In amoebae and in *Acetabularia*, the nucleus seems to be somewhat more active than the cytoplasm as regards the incorporation of amino acids into proteins; but again, a difference between the nucleus and the cytoplasm is never as strong as it is for RNA anabolism. In higher organisms, liver cells show a much faster incorporation of amino acids into nuclear proteins than into cytoplasmic proteins (Ficq and Errera, 1955; Moyson, 1955). However, liver cells are the exception rather than the rule, since Ficq and Brachet (1956) did not find any conspicuous accumulation of labeled phenylalanine in the nuclei of pancreas, intestine, lung, heart, muscle, kidney, spleen and uterus cells of the mouse. Labeling of nuclear proteins, methionine being used as a precursor, has recently also been reported by Pelc (1956). The nuclei show appreciable incorporation of the precursor even in tissues where mitotic activity is very small (thyroid, seminal vesicle, epididymis, nerve cells), but Pelc (1956) does not state whether the radioactivity of the nuclei is higher than that of the cytoplasm or not. There is one instance, however, in which the nuclei always show a much higher radioactivity than the cytoplasm after treatment with a labeled amino acid. This occurs, as already mentioned, during the early development of amphibian and avian embryos (Brachet and Ledoux, 1955; Waddington and Sirlin, 1954; Sirlin, 1955). This is not surprising since, in these embryos, we are dealing with very actively dividing cells; extensive synthesis of nuclear proteins is only to be expected under such circumstances.

It is interesting to note, however, that according to a recent autoradiographic study by Sirlin and Waddington (1956), incorporation of amino acids into proteins of chick embryos is highest in the nucleoli, the nucleolus-associated chromatin and the cytoplasm. Such conclusions are in obvious agreement with Caspersson's (1941, 1950) ideas.

On the other hand, in recent experiments, Carneiro and Leblond (1959) were unable to find any incorporation of tritium-labeled amino acids into nucleolar proteins of many cells.

In conclusion, present autoradiographic experiments suggest that there are considerable differences between various cells as far as protein metabolism is concerned. Except for rapidly dividing cells, protein anabolism is not necessarily stronger in the nucleus than in the cytoplasm. On the other hand, a very active RNA metabolism in the nucleus is the general rule. We shall now try to ascertain whether similar conclusions can be drawn from the merotomy experiments performed on *Amoeba proteus* and *Acetabularia mediterranea*.

b. Amoeba proteus

In *Amoeba proteus*, the removal of the nucleus is quickly followed by loss of motility; even after a few minutes, pseudopod formation becomes sporadic and the enucleate halves soon become spherical. They are unable to feed on living prey, in contrast to normal amoebae or nucleate halves, but they survive almost as long as the latter; if both are kept fasting, enucleate halves may survive for as long as 2 weeks, while nucleate ones die after 3 weeks.

In another species of amoebae *(A. sphaeronucleus)*, the effects of enucleation are similar. The interesting and delicate experiments of Comandon and De Fonbrune (1939) have shown that motility *(i.e.* pseudopod formation) is resumed in a truly dramatic manner when a nucleus is reintroduced into a cytoplasmic fragment which has been severed from the nucleus 2 or 3 days previously. If, however, the enucleate half comes from an amoeba which has been operated on 6 days before, the graft of a nucleus no longer has a favourable effect. Apparently, irreversible changes occur, sooner or later, in enucleated cytoplasm.

Very interesting also are the nuclear transfer experiments of Lorch and Danielli (1950) and Danielli *et al.* (1955) (see also Danielli, 1955, 1959). These workers have succeeded in exchanging nuclei between two distinct, but closely related, species of amoebae, *A. proteus* and *A. discoides.* The result is the production of "hybrids" in organisms in which no sexual reproduction is known to take place. They found that the nucleus of either species is capable of restoring locomotion activity in enucleated cytoplasm. The morphological characters of the "hybrids" *(e.g.* shape, size of the nucleus) show strong cytoplasmic dominance. The shape and locomotion are intermediate between those of the "parent" strains. As we shall see later, however, the nucleus exerts specific effects on the production of certain proteins. It is the belief of Danielli (1955, 1959) that the nucleus determines the specific character of the macromolecules, while the cytoplasm is more important in the organization of these macromolecules into functional units. One thing is clearly proved by these elegant experiments: there exist *mutual* interactions and exchanges between nucleus and cytoplasm. We shall soon find other instances in which the nucleus lies under cytoplasmic control. It would thus obviously be a mistake to believe that the control exerted by the nucleus on the cytoplasm is the only type of control in the cell.

After these introductory remarks on the biological effects of enucleation in amoebae, we shall now deal with the RNA and protein metabolism of nucleate and enucleate fragments.

Cytochemical observations with Unna staining show that the

basophilia of the enucleate fragments begins to decrease a couple of days after the section (Brachet, 1955). Even by the 5th day, the staining differences between the nucleate and enucleate halves are very conspicuous; the nucleate fragments become almost colorless in experiments of longer duration (Figs. 34, 35, p. 111). The cytological structure of the enucleate fragments is also changed: it is now finely granular rather than fibrillar after acid fixation. It is therefore likely that the removal of the nucleus exerts profound effects on the structure of the ergastoplasm. The decrease in basophilia probably corresponds to the disappearance or reduction in number of the ergastoplasmic "small granules"; the more granular aspect of the ground cytoplasm in the enucleate halves might represent distortion or breakdown of the ergastoplasmic lamellae.

Recent studies with the electron microscope (Brachet, 1959) have shown that amoebae do not possess a well-organized ergastoplasm. Nevertheless, removal of the nucleus makes the structure of the RNA-containing vesicles much coarser.

Quantitative estimations of the RNA content (Brachet, 1955) completely confirm the cytochemical observations. The nucleate halves maintain their RNA content constant, even after 12 days of fasting. In the enucleate cytoplasm, on the other hand, there is a steady and marked decrease in the RNA content; it drops by 60% within 10 days. These results have been confirmed by Prescott and Mazia (1954) and by James (1954). The latter claims, however, that the RNA content also drops when intact amoebae are kept fasting. Therefore, the loss of RNA might not be a direct consequence of enucleation; but it has been shown (Brachet, 1955) that the RNA content of fasting whole amoebae remains constant when they are kept under such experimental conditions that they do not markedly decrease in volume.

These experiments lead to the conclusion that in amoebae the nucleus exerts an important control on the maintenance of cytoplasmic RNA. Since, in amoebae, almost all of the RNA is localized in the microsome fraction, it can even be said that the small RNA-rich granules of the ergastoplasm lie under close nuclear control.

Our experimental data on the RNA content of nucleate and

enucleate *Amoeba* halves are obviously compatible with the idea that cytoplasmic RNA originates from nuclear RNA. They do not, however, prove that this is so, for RNA might disappear from enucleated cytoplasm for a variety of reasons other than that of a nuclear origin. More direct experiments have been designed by Goldstein and Plaut (1955) to prove the nuclear origin of cytoplasmic RNA. These workers labeled amoebae strongly with ^{32}P by feeding them with *Tetrahymena* cultivated in the presence of radiophosphate. The nucleus of the tagged amoebae was then removed and grafted into normal unlabeled amoebae or into enucleate halves. Autoradiographs showed clearly that the cytoplasm of the grafted amoebae becomes radioactive after 12 or more hours. Utilization of the ribonuclease test further showed that, under the conditions adopted for the autoradiography (fixation in 45 % acetic acid), all the autoradiographically detectable ^{32}P in both the nucleus and the cytoplasm is in the form of RNA. When the tagged nucleus is grafted into a whole amoeba so as to produce a binucleate cell, it is found that the originally unlabeled nucleus does not acquire any significant amount of radioactivity. This last experiment shows that the cytoplasm does not supply RNA to the nucleus, which, therefore, must synthesize its own RNA. Once synthesized in the nucleus, RNA can be transferred to the cytoplasm and the transfer proceeds in that direction only.

These experiments of Goldstein and Plaut (1955) are of far-reaching importance for our understanding of the interactions between nuclear and cytoplasmic RNA. They certainly deserve a short critical discussion. There is no doubt that Goldstein and Plaut (1955) have good evidence for the view that RNA is synthesized in the nucleus and transmitted therefrom to the cytoplasm. However, as pointed out by the authors themselves, they have not proved that the labeled material migrating to the cytoplasm is the RNA as it actually existed in the nucleus; it might be a precursor of a more or less complex nature. Goldstein and Plaut's (1955) demonstration, that the labeled RNA (or its precursor) which has been passed from the nucleus into the cytoplasm cannot be used for further nuclear RNA synthesis, does not seem entirely convincing.

Proof that the RNA transfer can only proceed in one direction, *i.e.* from the nucleus toward the cytoplasm, would be more complete if it had been shown that an unlabeled nucleus grafted in a *strongly* labeled enucleate cytoplasm never becomes radioactive. In Goldstein and Plaut's (1955) experiments on binucleate amoebae, the radioactivity of the cytoplasm seems to be rather weak and no unequivocal answer can be obtained from their observations.

An important additional remark was made by Goldstein and Plaut (1955) who noted that the possibility of the complete synthesis of *some* RNA in the cytoplasm is not ruled out by their data. In other words, besides a transfer of nuclear RNA to the cytoplasm, independent synthesis may occur in the latter. This seems to be probable in view of autoradiographic experiments performed in this laboratory by Skreb-Guilcher (1955). Studying the incorporation of labeled adenine in nucleate and enucleate *Amoeba* halves, she obtained a measurable incorporation into the RNA of enucleated fragments separated for 1 and 3 days. The activity of these fragments was, however, about four times less than that of the nucleate halves. The incorporation in enucleate cytoplasm became negligible when, 8 days after the section, its RNA content had dropped markedly. Similar results have been reported by Plaut and Rustad (1956) who studied the uptake of adenine into *Amoeba* fragments and found that it is an effective RNA precursor in this organism. Their experiments show that the presence of the nucleus is not essential for the uptake of adenine; but the nucleus is important for this uptake during the early incubation period, since the ratio between the nucleate and enucleate halves is 2.1 : 1.

More recently, Plaut and Rustad (1957) have reported results which agree perfectly well with those of Skreb-Guilcher (1955); using radio-active adenine as a label, they found that there is a mechanism of cytoplasmic incorporation into RNA which can operate in the absence of the nucleus.

Nevertheless, recent autoradiography experiments of Prescott (1957) lead to different results and conclusions. According to him, there is no incorporation whatsoever of labeled *uracil* in enucleate halves; the whole of cytoplasmic RNA would thus, in amoebae, originate from the nucleus.

The reason for this discrepancy is not yet clear, but it might simply be due to the fact that uracil is perhaps not as easily incorporated into RNA as adenine. In fact, the incorporation of adenine itself into the RNA of amoebae is disappointingly low and, for this reason, incorporation of $^{14}CO_2$ into RNA was studied. This precursor is very well incorporated into amoebae but its specificity is of course very low. The results obtained in this investigation (Tencer and Brachet, 1958; Brachet, 1959), in which both autoradiography and counting techniques were used, confirm the data previously obtained with adenine. Removal of the nucleus strongly reduces (by a factor of 2 to 3) the incorporation of $^{14}CO_2$ into RNA; but easily measurable incorporation of $^{14}CO_2$ into RNA can be detected even in fragments which have been devoid of the nucleus for 8 days. It is thus likely that some synthesis of RNA is still possible in the prolonged absence of the nucleus. Furthermore, the fact that such a simple precursor as carbon dioxide can be utilized by enucleate fragments clearly shows that very complex metabolic processes can go on in amoebae, even in the absence of the nucleus, for a considerable time.

The conclusion is that the nucleus of amoebae is of considerable importance for RNA metabolism; in its absence, the RNA content of the cytoplasm drops markedly. Since Goldstein and Plaut's (1955) work, there is good evidence that the nucleus actively synthesizes RNA and that nuclear RNA is transferred to the cytoplasm. But the cytoplasm is not entirely inactive, and a limited synthesis or turnover of RNA can continue in enucleate cytoplasm. Such a picture is, of course, in very good agreement with Mazia's (1952) replacement hypothesis.

If removal of the nucleus produces a marked weakening of RNA metabolism in *Amoeba*, one would expect a parallel inhibition of protein anabolism, if both are really closely linked together. In accordance with this expectation, the total protein content was readily found to drop more quickly in enucleate halves than in nucleate fragments (Brachet, 1955). This finding raised a new question: are all the cytoplasmic proteins of the *Amoeba* equally dependent on the nucleus?

This was studied (Brachet, 1955) by following, over a period of time, the changes of various enzymes (hence of as many specific proteins) in both types of fragments. The experiments showed that the removal of the nucleus results in widely different effects in the case of different enzymes. Some of them, like protease, enolase and adenosine triphosphatase, remain practically unchanged after the removal of the nucleus. Amylase (Urbani, 1952) behaves in much the same way, except for an unusual initial increase in activity in the enucleated halves. Dipeptidase, on the other hand, shows an initial decrease and then remains essentially constant. Acid phosphatase and esterase practically disappears from the enucleated cytoplasm after a few days. These experiments establish beyond doubt that different enzymes are placed under nuclear control to different extents and that this postulated "control" of the nucleus is much more complex than might have been expected. It should be noted that none of the enzymes studied ever showed a predominant nuclear localization, a finding which disposes of Wilson's (1925) theory of nuclear storage or synthesis of enzymes.

The reason for this strikingly different behavior of the various enzymes that we studied remains uncertain. It is tempting to speculate that the cellular localization of the different enzymes is of importance in this respect. As shown by Holter (1954, 1955), amylase and protease are bound to large granules in the *Amoeba* (mitochondria or the lysosomes of De Duve *et al.* (1955)). This might imply that mitochondria largely escape nuclear control, as indicated by the experiment made of the effects of enucleation on the respiration of amoebae. The different behavior of dipeptidase is not surprising since, according to Holter (1954), this ubiquitous enzyme is probably in solution in the hyaloplasm. Acid phosphatase and esterase, which behave like RNA, might be bound to microsomes. But this interpretation of the findings is weakened by Holter's (1955) more recent report that acid phosphatase behaves like protease: it is normally bound to large granules and is released in solution on homogenization. Protease, amylase and acid phosphatase might well be present in lysosomes, these baglike granules which apparently contain enzymes in solution, according to De Duve *et al.* (1955). Unequal resistance of the lysosomes to autolytic processes induced by the removal of the nucleus might explain all the results; such a hypothesis would also help to explain the temporary increase in activity of amylase in the enucleate halves. Nothing more definite than that can be said until more is known about the intracellular distribution of the hydrolytic enzymes in amoebae.

Recent experiments in the author's laboratory by Sells and Six (1959) on adenosine triphosphatase (ATPase) clearly show how complicated the situation can be. They confirmed our earlier finding that the activity of total ATPase remains unchanged after removal of the nucleus, even after 8 days. But they also followed the activity of the "ecto-ATPase", that is, the enzyme which is present in the membrane and which can be estimated by following the breakdown of ATP added to the medium. For normal amoebae and for nucleate fragments, identical values were obtained for total and ecto-ATPase; but, in the enucleate fragments, the ecto-ATPase activity decreased markedly (about 50% in 5 days) although, as mentioned above, the total ATPase activity remained unchanged. It might be that part of the enzyme normally localized on the membrane shifts to the interior of the cell upon removal of the nucleus.

Protein metabolism in fragments of amoebae has, of course, also been analyzed by studies on the incorporation of labeled amino acids. Mazia and Prescott (1955) carefully studied the incorporation of ^{35}S-methionine into the proteins of the two halves and found that the percent incorporation is lower by a factor of 2–5 in the enucleate half immediately after the cell has been cut into two. The ratio of the incorporation in the nucleate and the enucleate halves rose to values as high as 20 after a few days. Mazia and Prescott (1955) concluded that the nucleus is either the seat of a considerable proportion of the protein synthesis or that this nucleus-linked synthesis is very closely coupled with processes that are localized in the nucleus. But the experiments also show that the nucleus is not the exclusive center of protein synthesis in the cell.

Autoradiographic experiments of Ficq (1956) and Brachet and

Ficq (1956), who used ^{14}C-phenylalanine as a precursor instead of
[35]S-methionine, are in substantial agreement with those of Mazia
and Prescott (1955). However, the differences between the nucleate
and enucleate fragments were much less striking, the ratio between
them being in the neighborhood of 2 (instead of 20) on the tenth
day after removal of the nucleus. In fact, this difference is largely
due to higher incorporation in the nucleus than in the cytoplasm of
amoebae.

Finally, Tencer and Brachet (1958) and Brachet (1959), in their
study of the incorporation of $^{14}CO_2$ in amoebae, were able to compare this process in RNA and proteins. The result was that *RNA
lies under much closer nuclear control than proteins.* In all experiments, the removal of the nucleus had a stronger effect on the incorporation of the precursor into RNA than on that into protein.
Such a result is of course in keeping with the fact that in amoebae
enucleate fragments lose the larger part of their RNA, while the loss
in total protein is moderate.

We shall now see whether similar observations can be made on
Acetabularia. A few words will first be said about the biological
observations which have been made on this very interesting organism; we shall then examine its RNA and protein metabolism.

c. Acetabularia

By far the most important experimental work done on this organism
is that of Hämmerling and his co-workers (review by Hämmerling
in 1953). The life cycle of *Acetabularia mediterranea* is depicted in
Fig. 36 (p. 112). The alga is made of a chloroplast-containing stalk
and of rhizoids during most of its life. A single large nucleus, with
an extraordinarily developed and basophilic nucleolus, is located in
one of the rhizoids. Later, the tip of the stalk forms a "cap" or
umbrella which serves for the reproduction of the alga. When the
umbrella is almost completely formed, the nucleus breaks down and
small daughter nuclei spread through the whole alga (Schulze, 1939),
including the cap, where resistant forms (the "cysts") are formed.
These cysts contain a few nuclei and are surrounded by a thick
capsule. After a maturation period, they can be stimulated to ger-

Text continued on p. 112

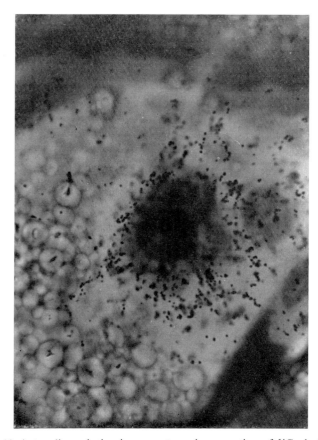

Fig. 32. Autoradiograph showing very strong incorporation of ^{14}C-adenin in the nucleolus of *Acetabularia* (courtesy of Dr. F. Vanderhaeghe).

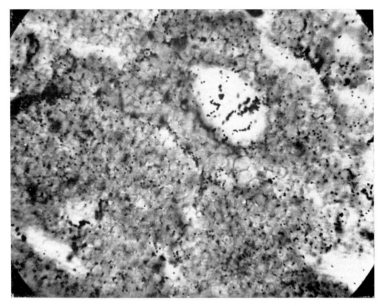

Fig. 33. High incorporation of labeled CO_2 into nuclei of amphibian gastrula (autoradiograph by Dr. A. Ficq).

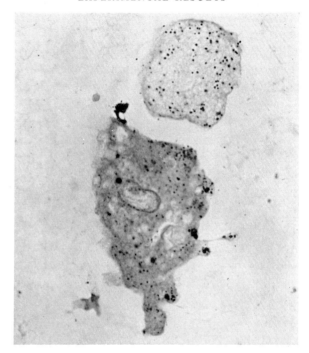

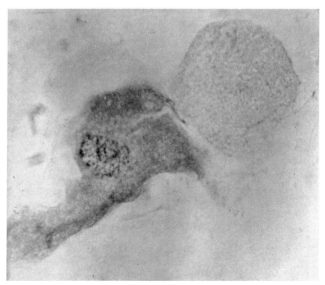

Figs. 34 and 35. Drop in basophilia occurring in enucleate fragments of amoebae (Brachet, 1955).

mination by short-time exposure to distilled water: the nuclei multiply and the cytoplasm divides. Flagellated gametes are produced and escape out of the broken cyst. Copulation of the gametes is quickly followed by the growth of the zygote, which soon differentiates into rhizoid and stalk. The whole life cycle takes about 5 months under laboratory conditions and 1 year in nature.

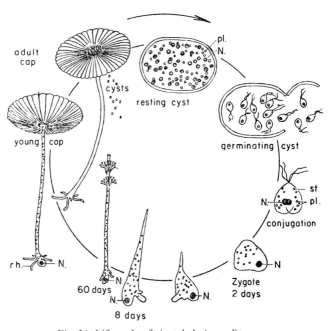

Fig. 36. Life cycle of *Acetabularia mediterranea*.

One of the main results obtained by Hämmerling (1934) is the demonstration that unnucleated stalks survive for a very long time (several months). Still more important is the fact that these enucleate parts are capable of important *regeneration*, including the formation of large-sized caps (Fig. 37, p. 121). It was concluded by Hämmerling, as early as 1934, that the morphogenetic capacity of an enucleate part is determined by the amount of nucleus-dependent morphogenetic substances stored in it; these substances are distributed along an anterio-posterior concentration gradient.

Further analysis of the problem by Hämmerling (1943, 1946) and his colleagues (Beth, 1943; Maschlanka, 1946) includes very interesting experiments on interspecific grafts. For instance, binucleate grafts containing one *A. mediterranea (med.)* and one *A. crenulata (cren)* nucleus form "intermediate" caps; trinucleate grafts containing two *cren* and one *med* nucleus give, as would be expected, caps which more resemble normal cren. If now an *enucleate cren* stalk is grafted with a *med* nucleate rhizoid, intermediate caps of various types are formed. If this first intermediate cap is removed, the new cap which forms is always a typical *med* cap. These results led Hämmerling (1953) to the following important conclusions. The nucleus-controlled morphogenetic substances show species-specificity; in binucleate grafts, distinct substances are produced by the two nuclei and intermediate caps of constant types are formed. In uninucleate grafts, the enucleate cytoplasm contains a store of morphogenetic substances of its own species; if this store is large enough, an "intergrade" cap is formed as a result of the competition between the substances stored in the enucleate piece and the substances produced by the grafted nucleus. Since the structure of the cap is obviously a hereditary character, it can be concluded (Hämmerling, 1953) that the substances produced under the influence of the nucleus are "products of gene action, which stand between gene and character". It should, however, be borne in mind that in these experiments it is not the nucleus *alone* which is transplanted: cytoplasm surrounding the nucleus is also grafted and it cannot be entirely excluded that cytoplasmic particles endowed with genetic continuity are also involved in the specific regenerative processes.

After this summary of the main facts concerning regeneration in *Acetabularia mediterranea*, we can now go into the RNA and protein metabolism of this organism.

Unfortunately, accurate RNA estimations are difficult to carry out in *Acetabularia*, which contains little RNA and a wealth of substances interfering with the assay methods. The first measurements, made by Brachet *et al.* (1955), indicated that there is a net synthesis of RNA in enucleate halves during the first week after removal of the nucleus. However, later work by Richter (1959) and by Naora, Richter and Naora (1959) failed to confirm this conclusion; these workers found that there is little change in the RNA content of enucleate fragments during the first weeks after operation. In any event, enucleate cytoplasm of *Acetabularia* markedly differs from enucleate fragments of amoebae where, as we have seen, removal of the nucleus is quickly followed by a marked drop in the RNA content. In *Acetabularia*, enucleate cytoplasm is capable of retaining its RNA store for a long time and to a surprising extent.

The reason for this marked difference between the alga and the amoeba might well be the presence of chloroplasts in the former. It has just been found by Naora, Brachet and Naora (1959) that RNA is still synthesized in the chloroplast fraction after removal of the nucleus; it decreases in the other fractions (microsomes and supernatant liquid), just as it does in amoebae. The contradictory results obtained in the past are probably due to the fact that various strains and culture conditions were used in the different experiments so that the importance of chloroplast multiplication was highly variable. At any rate, the conclusion of the last experiments made on this difficult material is that the total RNA content of enucleate fragments does not markedly change, but there is a net synthesis of chloroplast RNA at the expense of the RNA present in the other cell fractions.

It is therefore not surprising that the incorporation of orotic acid, a labeled precursor of RNA, remains very active in the absence of the nucleus (Brachet *et al.*, 1955). In fact, the incorporation is from the beginning 50% higher in the nucleate than in the enucleate halves, but there is no striking fall in the latter, even 70 days after the operation. This situation merely reflects the fact that the nucleus itself (in particular the large nucleolus) is the site of an especially active RNA metabolism (Stich and Hämmerling, 1953; Hämmerling and Stich, 1956; Vanderhaeghe, 1957). The more recent experiments of Naora, Brachet and Naora (1959) have confirmed that enucleate fragments can easily incorporate such precursors as ^{14}C-adenine and ^{14}CO$_2$ in their RNA. They further show that the alga is capable of synthesizing free adenine and guanine in the absence of the nucleus. Finally, these isotope experiments have confirmed that the synthesis of RNA is practically confined to the chloroplasts.

Thus, the present situation is as follows. RNA anabolism is predominant in the nucleolus, but the chloroplasts, which have often been believed to be cytoplasmic self-duplicating units, can synthesize RNA in the absence of the nucleus. The other cell fractions (microsomes, supernatant liquid) are, as in amoebae, dependent on the cell nucleus for the synthesis and even for the maintenance, of their RNA store.

It is thus probable that two distinct phenomena co-exist in *Acetabularia* as in *Amoeba*: independent cytoplasmic RNA synthesis (especially in the chloroplasts) occurs along with transfer to the cytoplasm of nuclear RNA.

In order to test the importance of RNA from nuclear origin for growth, morphogenesis and protein synthesis, ingenious experiments have been performed by Stich and Plaut (1958). They treated nucleate and enucleate fragments with ribonuclease for a few days and then returned them to normal sea water. After a while, the nucleate fragments started to regenerate and synthesize proteins; but nothing of the sort happened in the enucleate fragments. Stich and Plaut's (1958) conclusion is therefore that the integrity of RNA of nuclear origin is required to ensure regeneration and protein synthesis. Attempts to repeat these interesting experiments (Brachet, 1959 and unpublished) failed to give such definite results, the main difficulty being to avoid the infection of the ribonuclease-containing solution. It could, however, be confirmed that ribonuclease really penetrates into the algae and that it exerts a stronger inhibitory action on the regeneration of the enucleate fragments than on that of their nucleate counterparts. Furthermore, it was found by the author (unpublished) that 5,6 dichloro-β-D-ribofuranosyl-benzimidazole, a substance which strongly inhibits RNA synthesis in mammalian cells, has also a stronger inhibitory effect on the regeneration of the enucleate halves. Finally, it was observed that normal purine bases (especially adenine), which are so quickly incorporated into nucleolar RNA, strongly inhibit the growth of normal algae (Brachet, 1959).

References p. 133/135

Taken together, all these facts lend support to the hypothesis of Stich and Plaut (1958). As in other cells, RNA would be mainly built in the nucleus and part of the cytoplasmic RNA would be of nuclear origin. This part would be the more important in regeneration. On the other hand, it is certain that independent cytoplasmic RNA synthesis and turnover are quantitatively much more important in *Acetabularia* than in *Amoeba* and the main reason for this difference is that only the former organism contains chloroplasts.

Let us now consider protein metabolism in *Acetabularia*. In the course of regeneration in *Acetabularia*, the growth of the enucleate fragment is paralleled by increases in wet weight and in protein nitrogen (Vanderhaeghe, 1954; Brachet *et al.*, 1955). If regeneration occurs under *suboptimal* conditions in which the stalks increase in length but form no or few caps, the rate of protein synthesis is the same in the nucleate and in the enucleate pieces for 1 to 2 weeks. Protein synthesis then stops altogether and alterations of the chloroplasts begin; they retain their chlorophyll, but their proteins are partially degraded. In contrast, the small granules (microsomes) remain quantitatively unaffected during this second period (Vanderhaeghe, 1954).

If, as in the experiments of Brachet *et al.* (1955), the algae are operated on just before the formation of the caps and if the fragments are placed under *optimal* culture conditions, the enucleated pieces form a high proportion of caps. As a result, net protein synthesis is definitely *faster* in the enucleate halves than in the nucleate rhizoids (Fig. 37, p. 121). These experiments, which have been confirmed by Hämmerling *et al.* (1959), clearly show that the presence of the nucleus is not necessary for protein synthesis, although it is required for *prolonged* protein synthesis; this completely stops after 2 to 3 weeks, that is, when the growth of the cap has ceased. Therefore, in *Acetabularia*, the rate of protein synthesis is initially increased by the removal of the nucleus.

Of great interest regarding the role of the nucleus in protein synthesis are recent observations by Werz (1957) who has studied the effects of adding nuclei from either the *mediterranea (med)* or the *crenulata (cren)* species in nuclear transplant experiments. The main conclusion is that the addition of a homologous nucleus has no appreciable effect on protein synthesis. The rate of the latter is the same whether the alga contains two or a single nucleus from the same species. In the heterologous *med cren* combination, the *cren* nucleus speeds up protein synthesis, a fact which is in agreement with the observation that protein synthesis is faster in *Acetabularia crenulata* than it is in *Acetabularia mediterranea*.

The biochemical results just described are in good agreement with the observations of Beth (1953a) who showed, in *Acetabularia*, that the presence of the nucleus exerts an inhibitory effect on cap formation; this process is initially speeded up when the stalk is severed from the rhizoid just before the formation of the cap.

Extensive experiments by Beth (1953b, 1955) have disclosed another interesting fact. Cap production markedly depends on the amount of light received by the algae. Intense illumination produces algae which have a short stalk and a large cap; insufficient light supply results in the formation of very long algae with small caps. The phenomenon studied by Beth (1953b, 1955) also occurs in nature: algae collected in the Mediterranean a few feet deep are short and have large caps in July; those obtained by dredging or deep-diving have long stalks and smaller caps.

These observations by Beth (1953b) have led Brachet *et al.* (1955) to a study of the regenerative capacities of the enucleate fragments which had been left in the dark during increasing lengths of time prior to exposure to light in order to induce regeneration. The experiments showed that the same percentage of caps is obtained with the stalks which had been kept two weeks in the dark as with those which had been immediately illuminated. But the regenerative potencies of the algae which are kept in the dark for periods longer than two weeks soon decrease; they disappear after 4 weeks. It may be concluded that the substances of nuclear origin which are required for regeneration disappear at the same rate in the light and in the dark; their maintenance is apparently not linked with the energy supply in the cytoplasm.

The chemical nature of the substance responsible for cap formation in *Acetabularia* remains unclear. There is some evidence, however, that sulfur metabolism must be involved in this morphogenetic process. It was found that treatment of the algae with mercaptoethanol, a sulfhydryl-containing substance, completely inhibits cap formation. On the other hand, dithiodiglycol (which is the oxidized counterpart of mercaptoethanol and which thus contains a disulfide linkage) stimulates the formation of caps in enucleate stalks. At very low concentrations, p-chloromercuribenzoate, which is also a sulfhydryl inhibitor, also exerts a stimulatory effect on cap production. Finally, methionine and, to a lesser extent, ethionine also have a favourable effect on the formation of caps in enucleate fragments (Brachet, 1959.) It is thus likely that the formation or absence of a cap is linked to some enzymatic system, the activity of which is regulated by the sulfhydryl–disulfide equilibrium. It would be of interest to study this equilibrium under the conditions of illumination used by Beth (1953a, b; 1955) in order to modify the size of the caps.

In order to get a better insight into the mechanisms of protein synthesis in *Acetabularia*, Brachet *et al.* (1955) studied the incorporation of $^{14}CO_2$ in the proteins of nucleate and enucleate halves. It was found that the incorporation reaction proceeds at the same rate in both fragments for two weeks. At that time, incorporation becomes progressively less active in the enucleate halves than in the others; after 7 weeks, the incorporation in the proteins of enucleate stalks becomes 2.4 times less than in the nucleate rhizoids.

It can be concluded that the incorporation experiments entirely confirm the results obtained for net protein synthesis. They further show that, even when net protein synthesis has ceased in the enucleate pieces, protein turnover continues for several weeks in the absence of the nucleus.

The incorporation of $^{14}CO_2$ into the proteins of *Acetabularia*, as one would expect, requires light; it becomes negligible in the dark. Further indications that the process is closely linked to photosynthesis are found in the fact that the specific activity of chloroplastic proteins is 2 to 3 times higher than that of the other proteins.

A different situation is found when ^{14}C-glycine is used as a precursor; its incorporation has, unfortunately, not been studied in fragments. It is interesting that the glycine uptake and incorporation are not dependent on the presence or absence of light. In contrast to the results obtained with $^{14}CO_2$, the incorporation is stronger in the microsomes than in the chloroplast fraction. A comparison of the results obtained with $^{14}CO_2$ and with glycine suggests that *Acetabularia* possesses two biochemically different mechanisms for protein synthesis. One of them requires CO_2, light and chloroplasts; in the second, where an amino acid is the precursor, microsomes are more important than chloroplasts. Such a conclusion stands in perfect agreement with the work of *Beth* (1953b, 1955) who demonstrated that growth of the stalks requires less light than cap formation.

A few more observations pertaining to the protein metabolism in *Acetabularia* deserve mention. For instance, incorporation of ^{14}C-glycine into the proteins is 45 % inhibited when the whole algae are placed for 2 weeks in the dark. Another significant fact is that treatment of the algae with 10^{-3} *M* thiouracil—which acts as an inhibitor of RNA metabolism—also inhibits (30%) the incorporation of glycine into the proteins of whole algae. These observations strongly suggest that RNA is involved, as usual, in the protein metabolism of *Acetabularia*. This conclusion is shared by Werz (1957), who studied the effects of trypaflavine on regeneration in *Acetabularia*.

We have seen that in *Amoeba* different enzymes are unequally placed under nuclear control; what is the equivalent situation in *Acetabularia*? It is known (Brachet *et al.*, 1955) that, as in *Amoeba*, the enzymes which play a part in nucleotide metabolism and which are said to be accumulated in the liver nuclei (DPN-synthesizing enzyme, adenosine deaminase, nucleoside phosphorylase, guanase) are in concentrations too low to be detected. But it is interesting that aldolase is synthesized (40% increase) in the regenerating enucleate stalks at much the same rate as the total proteins (Baltus, 1959). In agreement with Stern and Mirsky's (1952) observations on isolated wheat germ nuclei, aldolase is concentrated in the nucleate half. However, it is not dependent on the presence of the nucleus for its synthesis in *Acetabularia*.

Recently, Hämmerling and his co-workers (1959) have studied a

References p. 133/135

number of enzymes in regenerating fragments of *Acetabularia*. They found that two enzymes involved in glucidic metabolism, like aldolase, are synthesized at the same rate as the total proteins; these enzymes are phosphorylase and fructosidase. On the other hand, they found a drop in acid phosphatase in regenerating enucleate fragments. It is interesting that this enzyme shows a strongly decreased activity after removal of the nucleus in *Amoeba* as well as in *Acetabularia*. It might be that acid phosphatase (and perhaps esterase) is synthesized in the nucleus itself or that the latter produces a substance which is absolutely necessary for the synthesis of this enzyme. It might also be that, in *Acetabularia*, the glycolytic enzymes which undergo synthesis in the absence of the nucleus are mainly localized in the chloroplasts, while acid phosphatase would be more closely linked to the microsomes. Such an explanation would be in conformity with the above-mentioned results of Naora, Brachet and Naora (1959) on the behaviour of chloroplastic and microsomal RNA's in regenerating enucleate fragments of *Acetabularia*. Obviously, a good deal more experimental work is required before a definite answer can be given to these intriguing questions.

The enucleate cytoplasm is thus still capable of synthesizing enzymes, that is, specific proteins. One would very much like to know whether induced enzyme synthesis is still possible in the absence of the nucleus. Unfortunately, the experiments designed to test that possibility (Brachet *et al.*, 1955) have not led to definite results. While an increase in catalase activity was found many times when enucleate pieces of *Acetabularia* were cultivated in the presence of hydrogen perodixe, it was impossible to repeat the results in later experiments. The reasons for this lack of uniformity in the results remain unknown; it might simply be due to bacterial contamination in the first series of experiments.

We have suggested before that the nucleus might successfully compete with the cytoplasm for RNA precursors. The same possibility exists for protein synthesis and there is even some evidence in its favour. It has been reported by Giardina (1954) and confirmed by Brachet *et al.* (1955) that the proportion of acid-soluble nitrogenous compounds, compared to protein nitrogen, increases

Text continued on p. 124

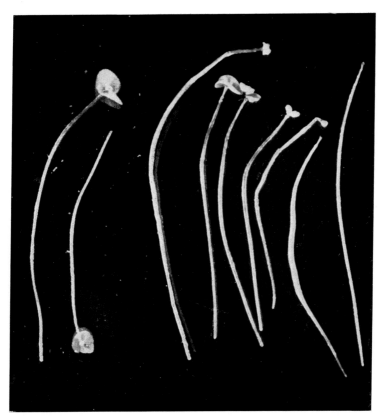

Fig. 37. Regeneration (cap formation) of enucleate stalks of *Acetabularia* (Brachet *et al.*, 1955).

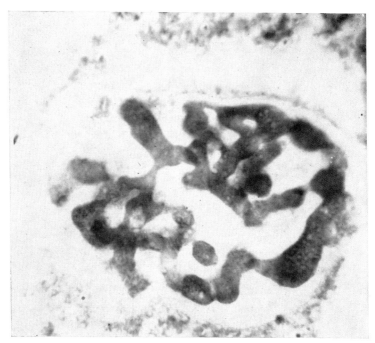

Fig. 38. Nucleus and nucleolus of normal *Acetabularia*. Unna staining
(Brachet *et al.*, 1955).

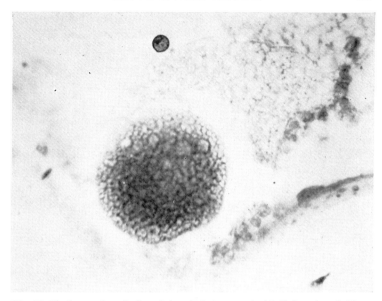

Fig. 39. Nucleus and nucleolus of *Acetabularia* treated with dinitrophenol. Unna staining (Brachet *et al.*, 1955).

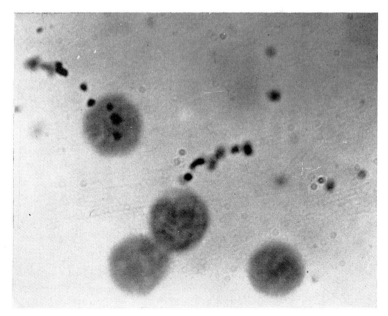

Fig. 40. Incorporation of labeled phenylalanine in isolated thymus nuclei. Autoradiographic method (A. Ficq).

much more in enucleate than in nucleate fragments. This increased synthesis of soluble nitrogenous compounds might correspond to an increase in the pool of the precursors for RNA and protein synthesis, when the competitive influence of the nucleus has been experimentally removed. A study of the chemical nature of this pool, which probably consists largely of amino acids, peptides and nucleic acids derivatives, might be rewarding; the analysis should be relatively easy by chromatographic methods.

Autoradiographic observations on the incorporation of labeled amino acids into nuclear proteins of *Acetabularia* (Vanderhaeghe, 1957) confirm the idea that considerable uptake occurs in the nucleus itself. The proteins of the nucleolus certainly become labeled to a measurable extent before those of the cytoplasm. But, as in amoebae, the difference in the incorporation activity between the nucleus and the cytoplasm is much less striking for the incorporation of an amino acid into proteins than for that of adenine into RNA.

Before we leave *Acetabularia* for other topics, a last and important remark should be made. We have mentioned many times in this chapter the control exerted by the nucleus on cytoplasmic activities; but it would be a mistake to forget that the nucleus also lies under cytoplasmic control. This fact has been shown very clearly by Stich (1951). If the algae are placed in the dark for some weeks, the volume of the nucleus and the nucleolus decreases; the latter becomes spherical instead of ribbon-shaped and loses much of its RNA. These changes are perfectly reversible when the algae are returned to light. Similar results have been obtained by Brachet (1952), when he treated algae with well-known poisons of oxidative phosphorylation such as dinitrophenol and usnic acid (Figs. 38 and 39, pp. 122 and 123). There is thus no doubt that energy production in the cytoplasm (by the chloroplasts and the mitochondria) is an essential factor for the regulation of the morphology and the chemical composition of the nucleus and, in particular, the nucleolus.

To summarize the above material, the experiments made on *Acetabularia* show that enucleate cytoplasm can retain its RNA content and synthesize proteins including specific enzymes. After removal of the nucleus, there is no change in the RNA content while there is a net synthesis of proteins; this indicates that, as in amoebae, the nucleus exerts a more direct control on RNA than on proteins. This can be explained if we assume that the nucleus is directly involved in the production of cytoplasmic RNA: protein synthesis would stop when the stock of RNA of nuclear origin is exhausted. We shall now see whether these ideas and conclusions are valid for other cells, e.g. reticulocytes and eggs.

d. *RNA and protein synthesis in the absence of the nucleus in reticulocytes and eggs*

The reticulocytes (immature red blood cells which have lost their nucleus and retained their RNA in the form of a basophilic network) have been extensively studied in Borsook's laboratory. It is now well-established (Borsook et al., 1952; Koritz and Chantrenne, 1954; Holloway and Ripley, 1952) that the reticulocytes are capable of incorporating amino acids into their proteins, including hemoglobin, despite the loss of their nucleus. In contrast, adult red blood cells have practically lost the ability to incorporate amino acids into proteins, and they contain traces only of RNA. According to Holloway and Ripley (1952), the development of reticulocytosis is accompanied by a substantial increase in the RNA content, which is closely paralleled by the amount of radioactive leucine incorporated into the proteins. The authors point out that their results are compatible with the view that RNA is closely associated with amino acid incorporation into proteins. It should be added that they are not compatible with the opinion that the cell nucleus is the most important center of protein synthesis.

Slightly different results have, however, been reported by Koritz and Chantrenne (1954), who found that the maximal rate of incorporation of labeled glycine precedes the RNA maximum by 2 or 3 days. The RNA peak coincides with the maximal content of the red blood cells in hemoglobin, dipeptidase and carbonic anhydrase. Since proteases, peptidases and phosphatases increase during reticulocytosis (Ellis et al., 1956), it is quite possible that the enucleate reticulocytes are capable of specific enzyme synthesis. In fact, some

References p. 133/135

experimental results of Nizet and Lambert (1953) readily show that an actual synthesis of hemoglobin occurs in reticulocytes. It should finally be added that autoradiographic observations by Gavosto and Rechenmann (1954) have shown that an excellent correlation between basophilia and incorporation of glycine into the proteins exists in reticulocytes: during the ripening of the erythrocytes, loss of basophilia and decrease in the incorporation go hand in hand.

Less is known about possible RNA synthesis in reticulocytes although recent isotope experiments of Kruh and Borsook (1955) indicate that they do incorporate radioactive glycine into their RNA.

The results obtained on reticulocytes are thus in full agreement with the data drawn from *Acetabularia*. The removal or spontaneous elimination of the nucleus does not necessarily lead to a rapid block of the mechanisms for RNA and protein synthesis.

Similar conclusions can be drawn from the few data that we possess for amphibian and sea urchin eggs, where the analysis has not as yet been pushed very far. In *Triton* eggs, Tiedemann and Tiedemann (1954) studied the incorporation of radioactive carbon dioxide into various chemical constituents, especially proteins and RNA. Working with eggs separated into two by ligation, they found no significant difference between the nucleate and the enucleate halves. In unfertilized eggs separated into "light" and "heavy" halves by Harvey's (1932) centrifugation method, Malkin (1954) observed a stronger incorporation of radioactive glycine into the RNA of the enucleate heavy halves than in the other. The difference was not so striking when Malkin (1954) studied the incorporation of the same precursor into the proteins. But the important fact remains that Malkin found considerable incorporation to occur in both the RNA and proteins of the enucleate egg fragments. It should be added, however, that these experiments of Tiedemann and Tiedemann (1954) and of Malkin (1954) can hardly be taken to prove that RNA and protein *synthesis* occurred in the absence of the nucleus. It is likely that net syntheses of protein and RNA are negligible in unfertilized eggs and that we are dealing, in fact, with a *turnover*. The latter obviously remains at its normal level in enucleate egg cytoplasm.

A recent autoradiographic study of Abd-el-Wahab and Pantelouris (1957) leads, however, to somewhat different results from
those which have just been described for sea urchin and newt eggs.
These workers found that the isolated polar lobes of the mussel
Mytilus (*i.e.* enucleate cytoplasm) show a considerable and rapid
decrease in the incorporation of amino acids and adenine in the
insoluble materials. No certain conclusion can be drawn from these
experiments, because the authors did not study the uptake and
concentration of the soluble precursors. It might well be that the
permeability of the polar lobe (which is known to differ strongly
from the rest of the cytoplasm by its viscosity and its low respiration)
to the amino acids and purines is abnormally low.

The present evidence shows that there are quantitative, rather
than qualitative, differences in the effects produced by nucleus
removal on RNA and protein metabolism. In *Acetabularia*, when
optimal conditions are chosen for regeneration, protein and perhaps RNA synthesis can be stimulated in enucleate fragments. The
synthesis of specific proteins, including probably hemoglobin,
whose synthesis is genetically controlled, apparently occurs in the
enucleate reticulocytes; the turnover of RNA and protein is not
affected by removal of the egg nucleus. In amoebae, the protein
and, especially, RNA synthesis and content decrease markedly in
enucleate fragments. In all cases, RNA is more affected by enucleation than protein, and the long-term effects of nucleus removal are
inhibitory for both protein and RNA anabolism.

A few words should now be said about results obtained by the
third method of study, *i.e.* the isolation of nuclei by centrifugation
of an homogenate.

e. General properties of isolated nuclei

The results of the many experiments in which precursors of either
RNA or protein were given to a living animal whose liver was then
homogenized and centrifuged can be summarized in a few sentences.
Since Marshak's (1948) and Jeener and Szafarz's (1950) pioneer
experiments, it has been repeatedly confirmed that, whatever the
precursor, incorporation proceeds much faster into nuclear RNA

References p. 133/135

than into cytoplasmic RNA. On the other hand, nuclear proteins, even the so-called "residual proteins" which are the most active proteins of the nuclei, incorporate labeled amino acids at a rate comparable to that found for mixed cytoplasmic proteins (Daly *et al.*, 1952; Allfrey *et al.*, 1955, Smellie *et al.*, 1953; etc.). Thus the residual proteins are less active than some of the cytoplasmic proteins, *e.g.* those of the microsomes. It can be concluded from this brief summary (see Brachet, 1957, for more details) that these *in vivo* experiments agree very well with all we have seen previously; the nucleus is more active and thus more directly involved in RNA than in protein synthesis.

Something should now be said about the very interesting *in vitro* experiments of Allfrey, Mirsky and their colleagues on protein synthesis in *isolated* thymus nuclei. These investigators found (1955, 1957) that if these nuclei are placed in a suitable medium, they actively incorporate amino acids into their proteins, especially in a protein fraction which is closely associated with DNA (Fig. 40, p. 123). Treatment of the nuclei with deoxyribonuclease breaks down part of the DNA and strongly inhibits the incorporation; but ribonuclease has no effect on this system. According to Allfrey and Mirsky (1957, 1958), the incorporation of amino acids in the proteins of nuclei partially depleted of their DNA content can be restored by the addition of unspecific DNA, of RNA and even of synthetic polynucleotides. The explanation of these puzzling results is that the incorporation process requires energy produced by phosphorylations in the nuclei themselves; these phosphorylations are inhibited when DNA is removed from the nuclei and are restored by the addition of polynucleotides. Finally, experiments in which various inhibitors were used showed that a synthesis of RNA in the isolated nuclei must precede the incorporation of the amino acids into the proteins. One can conclude from this work of Allfrey and Mirsky (1957, 1958) that the role of DNA in the synthesis of nuclear proteins is indirect rather than direct and that, as usual, RNA is somehow involved in this synthesis.

4. CONCLUSIONS

There is no doubt that protein synthesis, including synthesis of specific proteins such as hemoglobin or enzymes, is possible in the absence of the nucleus and, therefore, in the absence of DNA. One of the limiting factors in protein synthesis by enucleate cell fragments is the energy production. This explains why *Acetabularia*, which contains chloroplasts and is capable of perfect photosynthesis in the absence of the nucleus, is so much superior to *Amoeba proteus* in this respect. Enucleate fragments of amoebae are unable to feed and it is no wonder that no net protein synthesis can occur in them. Reticulocytes and enucleate egg fragments occupy an intermediary position between these two extremes. They are capable of appreciable protein synthesis or turnover but the reticulocytes are living in a nutrient medium and the egg fragments are supplied with large reserves of yolk. From this viewpoint, the variety of results obtained in enucleation experiments becomes logical and we arrive at the conclusion that the differences between enucleate fragments of *Amoeba* or *Acetabularia* are of a quantitative, rather than a qualitative, nature.

With regard to the relationships existing between the nucleus and the cytoplasm in the mechanisms of energy production, it is possible that the nucleus might produce co-enzymes required for glycolytic and oxidative reactions. In fact, there is some evidence for the view that diphosphopyridine nucleotide (DPN), as well as several other nucleotides, are synthesized in the nucleus (Hogeboom and Schneider, 1952; Baltus, 1955). On the other hand, we know that the main sites of energy production are located in the cytoplasm (mitochondria, chloroplasts) and we have seen that suppression of these cytoplasmic mechanisms of energy production have far-reaching consequences on the morphology and RNA content of the nucleolus in *Acetabularia*. Similar observations can be made on other cells, for example, on amphibian eggs treated with dinitrophenol. In conclusion, the nucleus depends on the cytoplasm for ATP production, but it might be a source of coenzymes for the cytoplasm.

References p. 133/135

But the main role of the cell nucleus is different. It is the main, if not the exclusive, site of *nucleotide synthesis* and not only of simple mono- and dinucleotides such as DPN, but also of the much more complex and important polynucleotides, DNA and RNA. There is growing evidence in the case of DNA in favour of the structure and mechanism of replication proposed by Watson and Crick (1953): DNA would be made of two complementary helices, which would separate from each other and reform their counterpart when DNA is synthesized. Thus DNA synthesis would be a function of DNA itself or, at any rate, of the chromosome. The mechanism of RNA synthesis remains more obscure but, as we have seen repeatedly in this chapter, synthesis of RNA is always much more active in the nucleus than in the cytoplasm and there is considerable evidence for the view that part at least of cytoplasmic RNA is of nuclear origin. It is very gratifying that the very different methods of investigation described in this chapter (autoradiography, work on enucleate organisms and work on homogenates) have yielded similar results and led to the same general conclusion: *the nucleus is the more important site of RNA synthesis.*

A logical consequence of such a conclusion is that the nucleus must exert a stronger control on cytoplasmic RNA synthesis (or maintenance) than on cytoplasmic protein synthesis. We have pointed out earlier that the nucleus exerts only a remote, indirect control on protein synthesis. This is exactly what would be expected if the nucleus produced an intermediary substance involved in protein synthesis; there is little doubt that this intermediary is RNA, from all the facts that have been presented and discussed in this book.

The results obtained from experiments on unicellular organisms are in good agreement with views which have been expressed repeatedly since Caspersson (1941, 1950) presented them first. DNA, which is the primary genetic substance, would synthesize RNA; proteins would, in turn, be synthesized under the influence of RNA. The template hypothesis provides an easy explanation for specificity. Specific DNA molecules (or parts of molecules) corresponding to each gene would act as a template for RNA; there would thus be as many specific RNA molecules as there are genes. Finally, each of these specific RNA molecules would act as a template for a specific protein, according to the mechanism discussed in Chapter 2. Such a scheme corresponds to the now familiar "slogan": DNA makes RNA, and RNA makes protein.

This catch-phrase, like all others, is an over-simplification, because it does not take into account the existence of nuclear and cytoplasmic RNA's and the possibility of independent cytoplasmic protein synthesis. The following scheme might perhaps help in the understanding of the proposed relationship between DNA, RNA and proteins in the different parts of the cell (see also Fig. 41).

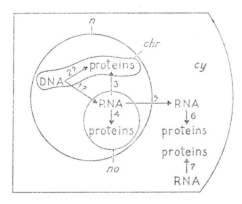

Fig. 41. Scheme proposing relationship between DNA, RNA and proteins in the different parts of the cell. chr: chromosomes; cy: cytoplasm; n: nucleus; no: nucleolus.

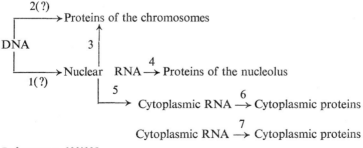

Step I (DNA makes RNA) is a logical one; but it must be admitted that there is no experimental proof so far for its existence. A question mark should thus remain for the time being.

With regard to steps 2 and 3, the recent experiments of Allfrey and Mirsky (1957) suggest, as already mentioned, that the role played by DNA in the synthesis of chromosomal proteins is an indirect rather than a direct one, and that the synthesis of these proteins is preceded by a synthesis of nuclear RNA. We should therefore consider step 3 as well established and step 2 as doubtful.

There is little information about the possible intervention of RNA in the synthesis of nucleolar proteins (step 4). The indirect evidence that we have to hand (cytochemical and autoradiography observations) is in favour of such a view. Experiments on the localized U.V. irradiation of the nucleolus, followed by autoradiographic studies of the incorporation of amino acids into nucleolar proteins, might give a more direct answer. Such studies are currently being made in the author's laboratory by Drs. Errera and Perry (1959). The first results indicate that destruction of nucleolar RNA exerts inhibitory effects on cytoplasmic RNA synthesis, but the effects on cytoplasmic protein synthesis are not yet known.

The last steps, 5, 6, 7, of the scheme have formed the main subject of this book and need not be discussed further. We have seen that part of the cytoplasmic RNA is of nuclear origin (step 5), but that autonomous synthesis of proteins and chloroplastic RNA (step 7) has been demonstrated in *Acetabularia*. Step 6 (the relationship between RNA and protein synthesis) was discussed in Chapter 1 and there is no need to repeat what was said there.

The scheme which we have presented remains obscure in many respects and should not be regarded in a dogmatic fashion; complicated as it looks, it is probably a considerable over-simplification of the reality. But it will serve a useful purpose if it can be used to test experimentally the various hypothetical steps, for one of the great mysteries of life will be solved when we understand the chemical relationships existing between the gene and the specific protein which is synthesized under its control.

ROLE OF THE CELL NUCLEUS

REFERENCES

ABD-EL-WAHAB, A. AND E. M. PANTELOURIS, (1957) *Exptl. Cell Research, 13*, 78.
ALLFREY, V. G. AND A. E. MIRSKY, (1957) *Proc. Natl. Acad. Sci. U.S., 43*, 589.
ALLFREY, V. G. AND A. E. MIRSKY, (1958) *Proc. Natl. Acad. Sci. U.S., 44*, 981
ALLFREY, V. G., M. M. DALY AND A. E. MIRSKY, (1955) *J. Gen. Physiol., 38*, 415.
ALLFREY, V. G., A. E. MIRSKY AND S. OSAWA, (1955) *Nature, 176*, 1042.
ALLFREY, V. G., A. E. MIRSKY AND S. OSAWA, (1957) *J. Gen. Physiol., 40*, 451.
BALTUS, E., (1955) *Arch. intern. physiol. et biochim., 64*, 124.
BALTUS, E., (1959) *Biochim. Biophys. Acta, 33*, 337.
BETH, K., (1943) *Z. Induktive Abstammungs u. Vererbungslehre, 81*, 252, 271.
BETH, K., (1953a) *Z. Naturforsch., 8b*, 334.
BETH, K., (1953b) *Z. Naturforsch., 8b*, 771.
BETH, K., (1955) *Z. Naturforsch., 10b*, 267, 276.
BORSOOK, H., C. L. DEASY, A. J. HAAGEN-SMIT, O. KEIGHLEY AND P. H. LOWY, (1952) *J. Biol. Chem., 196*, 669.
BRACHET, J., (1952) *Experientia, 8*, 347.
BRACHET, J., (1955) *Biochim. Biophys. Acta, 18*, 247.
BRACHET, J., (1957) *Biochemical Cytology*, Academic Press, New York.
BRACHET, J., (1959) *Exptl. Cell Research, suppl. 6*, 78.
BRACHET, J. AND A. FICQ, (1956) *Arch. biol. (Liège), 67*, 431.
BRACHET, J. AND L. LEDOUX, (1955) *Exptl. Cell Research, suppl. 3*, 27.
BRACHET, J., H. CHANTRENNE AND F. VANDERHAEGHE, (1955) *Biochim. Biophys. Acta, 18*, 544.
BRIGGS, R. AND T. J. KING, (1953) *J. Exptl. Zool., 122*, 485.
CARNEIRO, J. AND C. P. LEBLOND, (1959) *Science, 129*, 391.
CASPERSSON, T., (1941) *Naturwissenschaften, 29*, 33.
CASPERSSON, T., (1950) *Cell Growth and Cell Function*, Norton, New York.
COMANDON, J. AND P. DE FONBRUNE, (1939) *Compt. rend. soc. biol., 130*, 740.
CUTTER JR., V. M., K. S. WILSON AND B. FREEMAN, (1955) *Am. J. Botany, 42*, 109.
DALY, M. M., V. G. ALLFREY AND A. E. MIRSKY, (1952) *J. Gen. Physiol., 36*, 173.
DANIELLI, J. F., (1955) *Exptl. Cell Research, suppl. 3*, 98.
DANIELLI, J. F., (1959) *Exptl. Cell Research, suppl. 6*, 252.
DANIELLI, J. F., I. J. LORCH, M. J. LORD AND E. G. WILSON, (1955) *Nature, 176*, 1114.
DE DUVE, C., B. C. PRESSMAN, R. J. GIANETTO, R. WATTIAUX AND F. APPELMANS, (1955) *Biochem. J., 60*, 604.
ELLIS, D., C. E. SEWELL AND L. G. SKINNER, (1956) *Nature, 177*, 190.
ERRERA, M. AND R. PERRY, (1959) Private communication.
FICQ, A., (1955a) *Arch. biol. (Liège), 66*, 509.
FICQ, A., (1955b) *Exptl. Cell Research, 9*, 286.
FICQ, A., (1956) *Arch. intern. physiol. et biochim., 64*, 129.
FICQ, A. AND J. BRACHET, (1956) *Exptl. Cell Research, 11*, 135.
FICQ, A. AND M. ERRERA, (1955) *Biochim. Biophys. Acta, 16*, 45.

134   ROLE OF THE CELL NUCLEUS

GAVOSTO, F. AND R. RECHENMANN, (1954) Biochim. Biophys. Acta, 13, 583.
GIARDINA, G., (1954) Experientia, 10, 215.
GOLDSTEIN, L. AND W. PLAUT, (1955) Proc. Natl. Acad. Sci. U.S., 41, 874.
HÄMMERLING, J., (1934) Arch. Entwicklungsmech. Organ., 131, 1.
HÄMMERLING, J., (1943) Z. induktive Abstammungs- u. Vererbungslehre, 81, 114.
HÄMMERLING, J., (1946) Z. Naturforsch., 1, 337.
HÄMMERLING, J., (1953) Intern. Rev. Cytol., 2, 475.
HÄMMERLING, J. AND H. STICH, (1956) Z. Naturforsch., 11b, 158, 162.
HÄMMERLING, J., H. CLAUSS, K. KECK, G. RICHTER AND G. WERZ, (1959) Exptl.
     Cell Research, suppl., 6, 210.
HARVEY, E. B., (1932) Biol. Bull., 62, 155.
HOGEBOOM, G. H. AND W. C. SCHNEIDER, (1952) J. Biol. Chem., 197, 611.
HOLLOWAY, B. W. AND S. H. RIPLEY, (1952) J. Biol. Chem., 196, 695.
HOLTER, H., (1954) Proc. Roy. Soc. London, B 141, 140.
HOLTER, H., (1955) in: Fine Structure of Cells, Symposium 8th Congress of Cell
     Biology, Leiden, 1954, Interscience, New York, p. 71.
JAMES, T. W., (1954) Biochim. Biophys. Acta, 15, 367.
JEENER, R. AND D. SZAFARZ, (1950) Arch. Biochem. 26, 54.
JOHNSON, R. B. AND W. W. ACKERMANN, (1953) J. Biol. Chem., 200, 263.
KORITZ, S. B. AND H. CHANTRENNE, (1954) Biochim. Biophys. Acta, 13, 209.
KRUH, J. AND H. BORSOOK, (1955) Nature, 175, 386.
LOEB, J., (1899) Arch. Entwicklungsmech. Organ., 8, 689.
LORCH, I. J. AND J. F. DANIELLI, (1950) Nature, 166, 329.
MALKIN, H. M., (1954) J. Cellular Comp. Physiol., 44, 105.
MARSHAK, A., (1948) J. Cellular Comp. Physiol., 32, 481.
MASCHLANKA, H., (1946) Biol. Zentr., 65, 157.
MAZIA, D., (1952) in: E. S. G. BARRÓN, (ed.), Modern Trends in Physiology
     and Biochemistry, Academic Press, New York, p. 77.
MAZIA, D., AND D. M. PRESCOTT, (1955) Biochim. Biophys. Acta, 17, 23.
MOYSON, F., (1955) Arch. biol. (Liège), 64, 247.
NAORA, H., J. BRACHET AND H. NAORA, (1959) J. Gen. Physiol. (in the press).
NAORA, H., G. RICHTER AND H. NAORA, (1959) Exptl. Cell Research, 16, 434.
NIZET, A. AND S. LAMBERT, (1953) Bull. soc. chim. biol., 35, 771.
ODEBLAD, E. AND G. MAGNUSSON, (1954) Acta Endocrinol., 17, 290.
PELC, S. R., (1956) Nature, 178, 358.
PLAUT, W. AND R. C. RUSTAD, (1956) Nature, 177, 89.
PLAUT, W. AND R. C. RUSTAD, (1957) J. Biophys. Biochem. Cytol., 3, 625.
POTTER, V. R., G. C. LYLE AND W. C. SCHNEIDER, (1951) J. Biol. Chem., 190,
     293.
PRESCOTT, D. M., (1957) Exptl. Cell Research, 12, 196.
PRESCOTT, D. M. AND D. MAZIA, (1954) Exptl. Cell Research, 6, 117.
RICHTER, G., (1959) Biochim. Biophys. Acta, 34, 407.
SCHULZE, K. L., (1939) Arch. Protistenk., 92, 179.
SELLS, B. AND N. SIX, (1959) Arch. intern. physiol. et biochim., 67, 123.
SIEKEVITZ, P., (1952) J. Biol. Chem., 195, 549.
SIRLIN, J. L., (1955) Experientia, 11, 112.
SIRLIN, J. L., AND C. H. WADDINGTON, (1956) Exptl. Cell Research, 11, 197.

SKREB-GUILCHER, Y., (1955) *Biochim. Biophys. Acta, 17*, 599.
SMELLIE, R. M. S., W. M. MCINDOE AND J. N. DAVIDSON, (1953) *Biochim. Biophys. Acta, 11*, 559.
STERN, H. AND A. E. MIRSKY, (1952) *J. Gen. Physiol., 36*, 181.
STICH, H., (1951) *Z. Naturforsch., 6b*, 259, 319.
STICH, H. AND J. HÄMMERLING, (1953) *Z. Naturforsch., 8b*, 329.
STICH, H. AND W. PLAUT, (1958) *J. Biophys. Biochem. Cytol., 4*, 119.
TAYLOR, J. H., (1953) *Science, 118*, 555.
TAYLOR, J. H., (1954) *Genetics, 39*, 998.
TAYLOR, J. H. AND R. D. MCMASTER, (1955) *Genetics, 40*, 600.
TENCER, R. AND J. BRACHET, (1958) *Arch. intern. physiol. et biochim., 66*, 443.
TIEDEMANN, H. AND H. TIEDEMANN, (1954) *Naturwissenschaften, 41*, 535.
URBANI, E., (1952) *Biochim. Biophys. Acta, 9*, 108.
VANDERHAEGHE, F., (1954) *Biochim. Biophys. Acta, 15*, 281.
VANDERHAEGHE, F., (1957) *Thesis*, University of Brussels.
VERWORN, M., (1892) *Arch. ges. Physiol. Pflüger's, 51*, 1.
VINCENT, W. S., (1954) *Biol. Bull., 107*, 326.
VISHNIAC, W. AND S. OCHOA, (1952) *J. Biol. Chem., 198*, 501.
WADDINGTON, C. H. AND J. L. SIRLIN, (1954) *J. Embryol. Exptl. Morphol., 2*, 340.
WATSON, J. D. AND F. H. C. CRICK, (1953) *Nature, 171*, 737, 964.
WERZ, G., (1957) *Experientia, 13*, 79.
WILSON, E. B., (1925) *The Cell in Development and Heredity*, Macmillan, New York.
WOODS, P. S. AND H. S. TAYLOR, (1959) *Lab. Invest., 8*, 309.
WRIGHT, S., (1945) *Am. Naturalist, 79*, 289.
ZALOKAR, M., (1959) *Nature, 183*, 1330.

Subject Index

in enucleation experiments, 95,
96, 98–100, 104, 105, 108, 124
on gradients in protein synthesis, 87
on lithium distribution in treated
gastrulae, 69
Avian pest, 42
Axolotl, 59
8-Azaguanine, 28
Azide, 44

Bacillus megaterium,
protoplasts, 32
sensitivity to RNase, 41, 42
Bacteria,
RNA content, 4, 7, 8
RNA, DNA and protein synthesis
in, 17–19
Basophilia,
correlation between,
and amino acid incorporation, 5,
126
and RNA content, 7
effects of enucleation on, 102
of RNase-treated cells, 38–41
β-Benzimidazole, effects of, on regeneration in enucleated Acetabularia,
115
Bile salts, for isolation of "small ribonuclein particles", 20
Brain, RNA content, 7

Calcium ions, associated with ribonucleoproteins in intercellular matrix, 85
Cancer, interest of RNase in the
chemotherapy of, 41
Cap formation, in enucleated Acetabularia, 117, 118
Carbon dioxide (CO_2) incorporation,
gradients of, during development,
65
into RNA and proteins after enucleation, 105, 114, 118, 119, 126
Catalase, induced synthesis, 19, 31,
120
Cellophane membrane, effects on induction, 82–84, 87

Cells,
dissociation, 80, 85, 88
follicle (see Follicle)
matrix uniting, 80, 84, 85
membrane of,
pinocytosis by (see Pinocytosis)
role in induction, 83–85
Centrifugation, effects of, on morphogenesis, 70, 71
Chick,
gradients of RNA in eggs of, 66
incorporation in,
of amino acids into nuclear proteins, 100
of glycine into microsomes, 21
inhibition of development by synthetic nucleosides, 68
p-Chloromercuribenzoate, 118
Chloromycetin, 8
Chloroplasts,
amino acid incorporation into, 23,
25
control of nucleus by, 124
RNA synthesis by, after enucleation, 114, 115
Chromosomes,
lampbrush (see Lampbrush)
replication, 130
Ciliates, impermeability to RNase, 41
Cleavage, in absence of nucleus, 88
Co-enzymes, production of, by nucleus, 129
Competence, 60, 69
Conditioned medium, 59, 86
Connective tissue, amino acid incor-
poration in, 6
Conversion hypothesis, 2
Cortex, of eggs, 85
Cyanide, 44
Cystine, incorporation, into micro-
somes, 21
Cytidine triphosphate, 24
Cytolysis, sublethal, 77, 86

Deoxycholate, for isolation of small
ribonuclein particles, 20, 22
Deoxyribonuclease (DNase), effects
of, on chloroplasts, 32